Front Cover: Elk Mountains, Maroon Bells, Just South of Aspen, CO

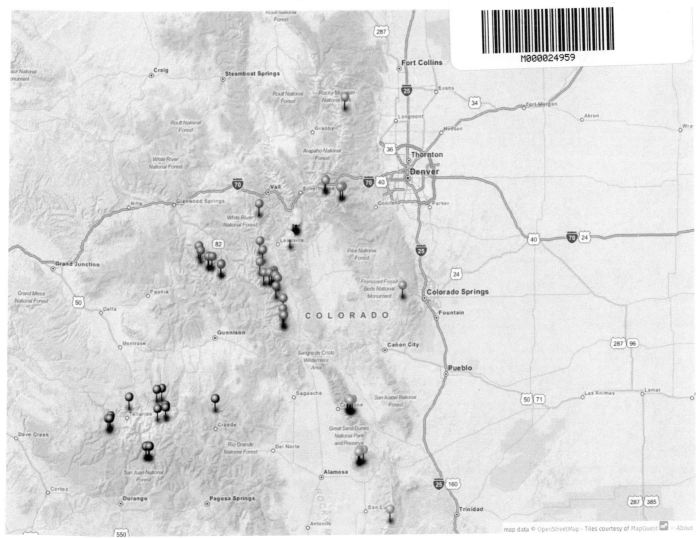

Map of Colorado Mountains Over 14,000 Feet (Fourteeners)
Red: Front Range
Yellow: Mosquito Range
Green: Sawatch Range
Orange: Sangre de Cristo Range
Blue: Elk Mountains
Black: San Juan Mountains

Above the Summit: An Antique Airplane Conquers the Colorado Fourteeners

ISBN: 0692286136
ISBN-13: 978-0692286135

Library of Congress Control Number: 2014915685

Published by Tenmile Publishing LLC
Breckenridge, CO

Website: garrettfisher.me

All photos in this book are available as prints, digital files, and framed prints. Please visit the website.

Table of Contents

Colorado Map of Fourteeners by Range   1

Index   3

Mountain Mystique   4

Mosquito Range   5

Mechanics of a 14er   15

Front Range   17

Elk Mountains   27

Flying in the Rocky Mountains   45

Sawatch Range   47

My Mountain Flying Experience   82

Sangre de Cristo Range   87

San Juan Mountains   107

Index

Mountain	Elevation	Range	Rank	Page-Compass Direction-Placement In Photo
Capitol Peak	14,130'	Elk Mountains	31	36-NW-Rear Right, 41-NW-Rear, 42-N, 44-NE
Castle Peak	14,265'	Elk Mountains	12	28-S-Center, 30-SE-Rear, 31-SE-Distant
Conundrum Peak	14,060'	Elk Mountains	40	28-S-Right, 30-SE-Front, 31-SE-Distant
Maroon Peak	14,156'	Elk Mountains	26	34-SW-Rear, 36-NW-Front Left, 38-S-Right, 40-SW-Left
North Maroon Peak	14,014'	Elk Mountains	55	34-SW-Rear, 36-NW-Front Right, 38-S-Right, 40-SW-Right
Pyramid Peak	14,018'	Elk Mountains	51	32-SE, 34-SW-Left Front, 38-S-Left
Snowmass Peak	14,092'	Elk Mountains	33	36-NW-Rear Left, 41-NW-Front
Grays Peak	14,270'	Front Range	9	20-E-Right
Longs Peak	14,255'	Front Range	15	22-E
Mt. Bierstadt	14,060'	Front Range	41	24-E-Right, 26-E-Right, 26-W-Background
Mt. Evans	14,264'	Front Range	14	24-E-Left, 26-E-Left, 26-W-Summit, 26-N-Summit
Pikes Peak	14,110'	Front Range	32	18-SE
Torreys Peak	14,267'	Front Range	11	20-E-Left
Mt. Bross	14,172'	Mosquito Range	23	11-NW
Mt. Cameron	14,238'	Mosquito Range	17	14-SE-Background
Mt. Democrat	14,148'	Mosquito Range	30	14-SE, 14-SE-Right
Mt. Lincoln	14,286'	Mosquito Range	8	14-SE Left
Mt. Sherman	14,036'	Mosquito Range	49	12-S
Quandary Peak	14,265'	Mosquito Range	13	6-NW-Background, 7-N, 8-SW, 10-SW, 10-SE
El Diente Peak	14,159'	San Juan Mountains	25	124-SSE-Center Rear, 126-SE-Center Rear
Handies Peak	14,048'	San Juan Mountains	43	114-S-Rear Center Left, 117-SE
Mt. Eolus	14,083'	San Juan Mountains	34	120-E-Right, 122-E-Center Right
Mt. Sneffels	14,150'	San Juan Mountains	29	128-N, 130-N, 131-NE
Mt. Wilson	14,246'	San Juan Mountains	16	124-SSE-Left, 126-SE-Left Rear
North Eolus	14,039'	San Juan Mountains	47	120-E-Right, 122-E-Center Left
Redcloud Peak	14,034'	San Juan Mountains	50	118-NE-Rear Center Left
San Luis Peak	14,014'	San Juan Mountains	54	108-NE-Left Rear
Sunlight Peak	14,059'	San Juan Mountains	42	120-E-Rear, 122-E-Rear Left
Sunshine Peak	14,001'	San Juan Mountains	58	118-NE-Rear Center Right
Uncompahgre Peak	14,309'	San Juan Mountains	6	110-SW-Center, 112-SSW
Wetterhorn Peak	14,015'	San Juan Mountains	53	110-SW-Center Rear, 114-S, 116-SSE
Wilson Peak	14,017'	San Juan Mountains	52	124-SSE-Center, 126-SE-Front, 127-S-Distant
Windom Peak	14,082'	San Juan Mountains	35	120-E-Rear, 122-E-Rear Center
Blanca Peak	14,345'	Sangre de Cristo Range	4	95-SE-Rear Right, 98-SE-Ctr Rear, 100-NE-Ctr, 102-NW-Ctr
Challenger Point	14,081'	Sangre de Cristo Range	36	90-E-Left, 94-SE-Distant
Crestone Needle	14,197'	Sangre de Cristo Range	19	90-E-Center Rear, 92-E-Center Left, 94-ESE-Distant
Crestone Peak	14,294'	Sangre de Cristo Range	7	90-E-Center Rear, 92-E-Center Right, 94-ESE-Distant
Culebra Peak	14,047'	Sangre de Cristo Range	44	104-E, 106-SE
Ellingwood Point	14,042'	Sangre de Cristo Range	46	95-SE-Ctr, 98-SE-Ctr Rear, 100-NE-Ctr Left, 102-NW-Rear Right
Humboldt Peak	14,064'	Sangre de Cristo Range	39	90-E-Left Rear, 92-E-Left Rear, 94-ESE-Distant
Kit Carson Peak	14,165'	Sangre de Cristo Range	24	90-E-Center, 94-ESE-Distant
Little Bear Peak	14,037'	Sangre de Cristo Range	48	98-SE-Right Rear, 100-NE-Front, 102-NW-Left
Mt. Lindsey	14,042'	Sangre de Cristo Range	45	95-SE-Rear Left, 98-SE-Rear Left, 100-NE-Center Rear
Huron Peak	14,003'	Sawatch Range	57	58-NW
La Plata Peak	14,336'	Sawatch Range	5	55-S, 56-SW
Missouri Mountain	14,067'	Sawatch Range	38	62-SW-Rear
Mt. Antero	14,269'	Sawatch Range	10	76-S, 78-S
Mt. Belford	14,197'	Sawatch Range	21	60-SE-Right, 62-SW-Center
Mt. Columbia	14,073'	Sawatch Range	37	66-E, 68-NW-Front, 69-SSW
Mt. Elbert	14,433'	Sawatch Range	1	52-N, 54-N, 55-NW
Mt. Harvard	14,420'	Sawatch Range	3	60-SE-Rear, 62-W, 63-W, 64-SSW, 68-NW-Rear
Mt. Massive	14,421'	Sawatch Range	2	49-NE, 50-NW
Mt. of the Holy Cross	14,005'	Sawatch Range	56	48-WSW, 49-NW
Mt. Oxford	14,153'	Sawatch Range	28	60-SE-Center, 62-SW-Front
Mt. Princeton	14,197'	Sawatch Range	20	70-S-Rear, 72-NW, 73-E, 74-SSE
Mt. Shavano	14,229'	Sawatch Range	18	79-SSW-Center Rear, 80-SSW-Center
Mt. Yale	14,196'	Sawatch Range	22	70-S
Tabeguache Peak	14,155'	Sawatch Range	27	79-SSW-Center Right, 80-SSW-Front
Sangre de Cristo Range				88-SE
Great Sand Dunes National Park				96-SE

Mountain Mystique

Most places on this planet have a single defining feature that dominates the perception of outsiders and identity of those who live there. For California, its nice weather, sunshine, and beaches. For Alaska, it's the raw wilderness and cold. New York City, the buzz of Manhattan. In the case of Colorado, the Rocky Mountains define the state in a broad sense. Visitors identify with the snow-capped peaks and locals spend their time embedding outdoor activities and mountain recreation into their lifestyles. The penultimate manifestation of the identity of the state lies in the highest peaks: mountains over 14,000 feet, otherwise known as "14ers" (fourteeners).

Sangre de Cristo Mountains

Fourteeners are superlative displays of what mountains mean. Forlorn peaks stand defiantly in the sky, shrouded in snow, clouds, and wind, and advertising their defiance of human encroachment. Out of touch of development and human habitation, these spires and towers of rock stand in a sky normally dominated by weather and stake their claim, denying both humans and the sky itself from their space. There is something mystical about them, a space the world over occupied by air and transient clouds, instead occupied by simple rock. We have 14,000' altitudes all over the planet, above every one of us. We can fly in those areas and measure them with instruments, or build antennas and towers into the sky. We feel little when climbing through that altitude in a commercial airliner, most notice the beverage service coming through or the pre-landing cabin preparations more so than what is going on outside. Yet, when a mountain stands in that spot and occupies it, our attention, imagination, and for some, our yearning, points toward that pile of rocks and fixates on it.

Gore Range

We have schools of higher learning dedicated to training scientists to study the geography, geology, and meteorology of these mountains. Humans naturally are curious as to how the mountains got there, how old they are, what kind of rock they are made of, if they are volcanic, if they are growing or eroding, if it can be climbed, what animals live on it, what the weather is like at the top. Conversely, what happens at 14,000' in the atmosphere above us is extremely important in our daily lives, with tremendous weather features, radio waves, and other natural phenomena occurring. Meh, we don't care. Leave that to the science nerds. The dichotomy is mystifying and seems to be eternal, as providing knowledge of these mountain ranges and features does not satisfy curiosity. In fact, it makes it worse as scores of people make pilgrimages to stand on the top of these giants, a feat of poetry and spirituality, where people engage in elevated levels of risk, exposure to hypoxia, and tremendous physical effort to get a fleeting sensation of standing on some of the highest mountains in the continental US.

What drives people to climb such mountains, tourists to slam on the brakes in their cars and pull over to gaze at them, or me to circle them in an airplane is rooted in the same thing: the enigmatic mystique of a pile of rocks that defies the conventions we live in on a daily basis. The top of a mountain means different things to different people. To me, it is the freedom of getting away from all confines: no trees, buildings, roads, nothing stands in my way at the summit. To others, it tells them where they cannot go. For yet others, it is a symbol of where no one can go. And for adventurers, it is an invitation to defy. Standing along side one person who views a mountain and appreciates the boundary, another person sees something that demands conquering. A mountain is many things to many people, something universal in that it captivates our wonder and yet universal in that there is no standard to what it represents. There are a few that hate them, thought I doubt they are reading this book unless they are engaging in literary penance.

Few in this world will stand on top of a 14er. Many will view them from a distance, or from the top of a hill after getting off a ski lift. Millions glance at Longs Peak from the Denver area. All of these perspectives are common, distant, and reduce a 14er to "ordinary" – another mountain with some snow on it. The depth of mystique and introspection possible from experiencing them is lost as what is not understood is dismissed. This book turns the tables on the 14ers, taking the almost forbidden and looking at them in ways even fewer people have the chance to: close up, nearby, above them. An airplane joins a 14er in its domain; the high reaches of the atmosphere, looking at the highest mountains in the continental United States as an equal. The goal is to bring the depth of these mountains to many who could not appreciate it otherwise, and to encourage an expanded understanding.

Peak 1

Mosquito Range

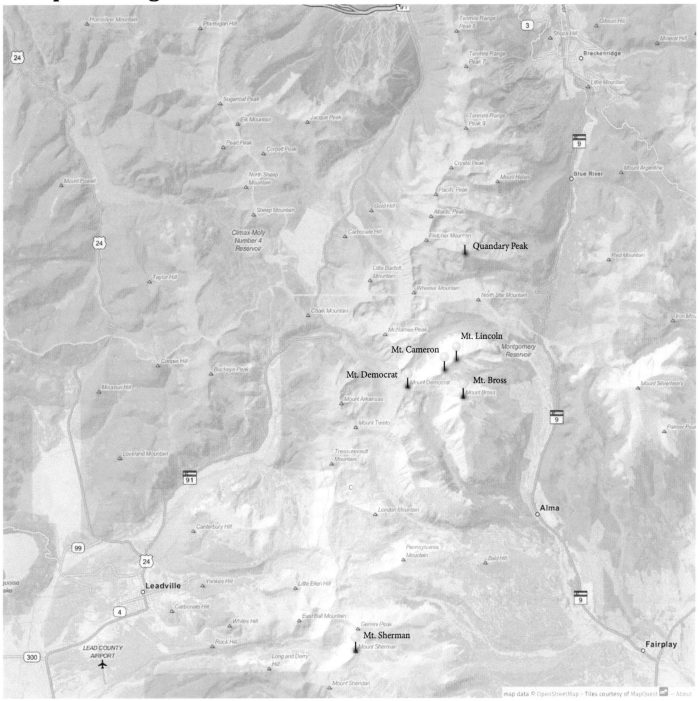

Page 8 & 9	SW	Quandary Peak
Page 10 (Top)	SSW	Quandary Peak
Page 10 (Bottom)	SE	Quandary Peak (Left)
Page 11	NW	Mt. Bross (Center), Mt. Democrat (Rear Left), Mt. Cameron (Center Rear), Mt. Lincoln (Rear Right)
Page 12 & 13	S	Mt. Sherman
Page 14 (Top)	SE	Mt. Democrat (Front), Mt. Cameron (Rear Center)
Page 14 (Bottom)	SE	Mt. Lincoln (Left), Mt. Cameron (Rear Center), Mt. Democrat (Right)

The entire Colorado 14er experience, over a 10-year period, started and ended with the Mosquito Range, Quandary Peak to be specific. First sighted while on a Colorado road trip (funded by state unemployment benefits) in 2005, I had an eccentric close friend with me who insisted on getting his picture taken in front of Quandary Peak. This solely had to do with his fetish for elongated words beginning with "Q." We then parked at Hoosier Pass and immersed ourselves in hypoxia, hiking in the snow to 12,200' and getting wind burned in 8-degree temperatures with gusts to 45mph, having not much of a clue what we were doing. I was in heaven; he was a muttering idiot with deteriorating brain function due to altitude sickness. "You wait here out of the wind while I finish the climb. Don't fall off the edge in your stupor." I came back

Hike west of Hoosier Pass (12,200'). Quandary Peak in the background.

only to find him in the fetal position, for which my dogmatic barking roused him from what was probably cerebral edema. He shook it off with a quad caramel macchiato at Starbucks in Breckenridge. The monastic, masochistic "mountain+Breck Starbucks" experience would later become a routine, where I would expose myself to death frequently and top it off with a warm latte.

Fast forward to my residency in Breckenridge 8 years later, and Quandary was somewhat of a fixation. I made the Hoosier Pass climb many times since, one across the valley involving search and rescue (I was the rescued, not a valiant civil volunteer), and one day I went to the top of North Star Mountain, the terminus of the Hoosier Pass route, at 13,500'. This put me staring at Quandary and Mt. Lincoln, two 14ers, almost like an equal. Each time, photos were sent back east to the Q literary fetishist, and we would reminisce on our short hike like it was the "good old days," even though I was enjoying the better days right then. It may have had more to do with the thrill of our ignorance, youth, and fiscal insolvency.

View of Hoosier hike, North Star Mountain, Quandary Peak (left to right) from across Hoosier Pass (13,100'). Breckenridge just out of view to the right.

Consistent with ongoing ignorance of the area, I discovered that one could drive to the top of the original Hoosier Pass hike (only after walking it a number of times), made under the duress of hypoxia and stupidity. One August night, we drove up, at quite the risk of death if a wrong turn was made off a cliff, to view the Perseid Meteor shower. Year after year in upstate NY we tried to view the meteorites, hosed by poor weather, full moons, poor meteorite performance, and the like. This night presented the stars to me in a way I could not ever imagine. With thunderstorms lighting the horizon from over 100 miles away, it was a sight that will change anyone that gets the chance to enjoy it.

I used to think that there couldn't possibly be much of a danger of predatorial animals above the timberline. What could their purpose be? On my evening hike to Northstar Mountain, I was enjoying my descent at 12,800' while listening to a glorious Vivaldi symphony in my headphones. Miles from civilization and "safely" above the timberline, I was quite content that I would not be stalked by anything nefarious. Of course, in the *rare* instance that I actually listen to headphones in the wild, I see an open jaw with teeth out of the corner of my eye. Quite unsettled (I jumped at least a foot into the air), it was a fox, which I could not tell at first glance if it was hungry, rabid, or curious. After being circled a few times (reminscient of mythological wolf packs circling their prey), I realized he wanted a handout. Out of ecological benevolence and stewardship, I would not feed him, though his cute look asked for it. He moved on and trotted up the trail toward the summit.

View of Quandary Peak from North Star Mountain (13,500')

The whole Colorado and 14er experience closed with Quandary Peak, without any particular planning, just a function of chance. It was the last 14er I took a picture of and flew past, on my way to more adventures as I went to Yellowstone and then across the continent to the east. There is the logical question of why someone would leave such a place being that we lived a 20 minute drive up the valley from Hoosier Pass, and the answer is as complex as the philosophy of our individual existences. Winter is extraordinarily long living at 9,600', with the first-to-last accumulating snowfall generally spanning a 9 month period. While the beauty on these pages opens the minds of those enjoying it who have never contemplated such a location, it is a viable risk that the length of winter can close the mind instead. Mountains are spires of beauty inviting challenge in the summer, and in the winter they digest humans that don't have an extremely atypical approach to scaling them. The Rockies push a person to grow on an individual level, and they do it about as fast as one can imagine. It would be entire biography to recount what over a year of living near the timberline does to expand horizons and grow.

Fox on North Star Mountain (12,800')

In our case, we found that growth now would be found elsewhere. When flying past Quandary Peak for the last time, it was a sense of accomplishment and not one of negativity. The sense of achievement presented an eye-opening concept to me, something largely foreign to American culture. We commonly associate our identities with the city in which we live, the house we own, and the job we have. Instead of individuals with an unmatchable uniqueness, we classify ourselves by simplistic externals, giving authority over our self-evaluation to the people around us. By having spent time here and choosing to leave, it occurred to me that it is not the location that defines us, its who we choose to be. Colorado is one amazing chapter in a story that keeps getting more interesting.

Milky Way from Hoosier Pass hike (12,200')

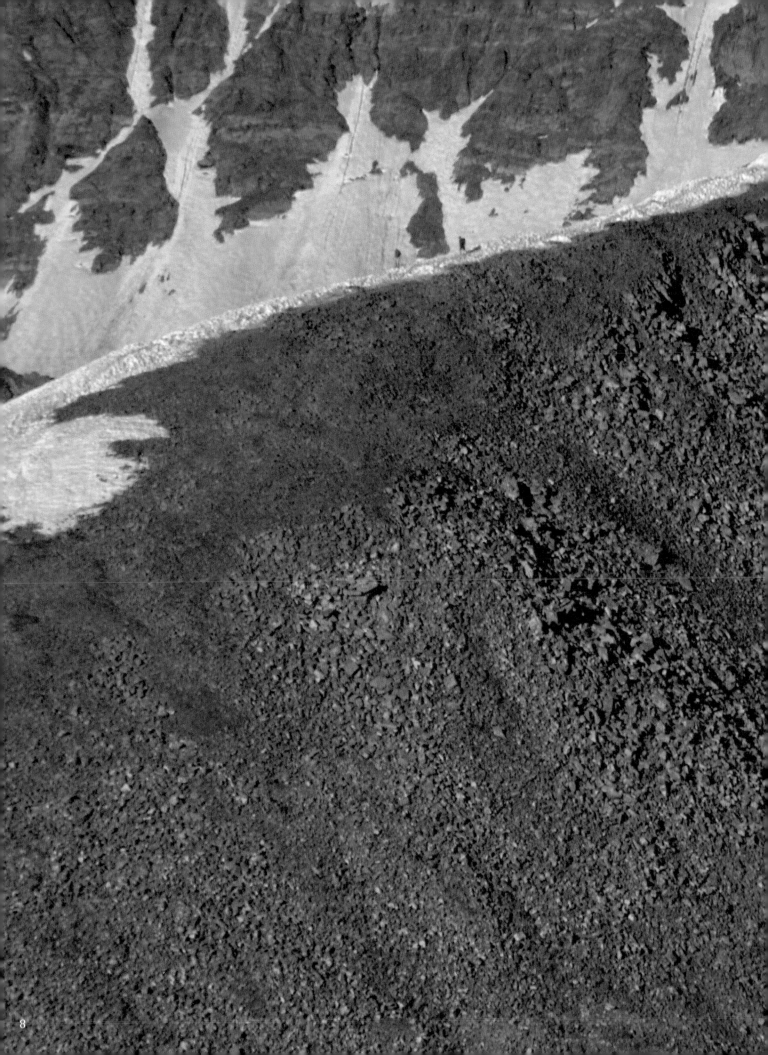

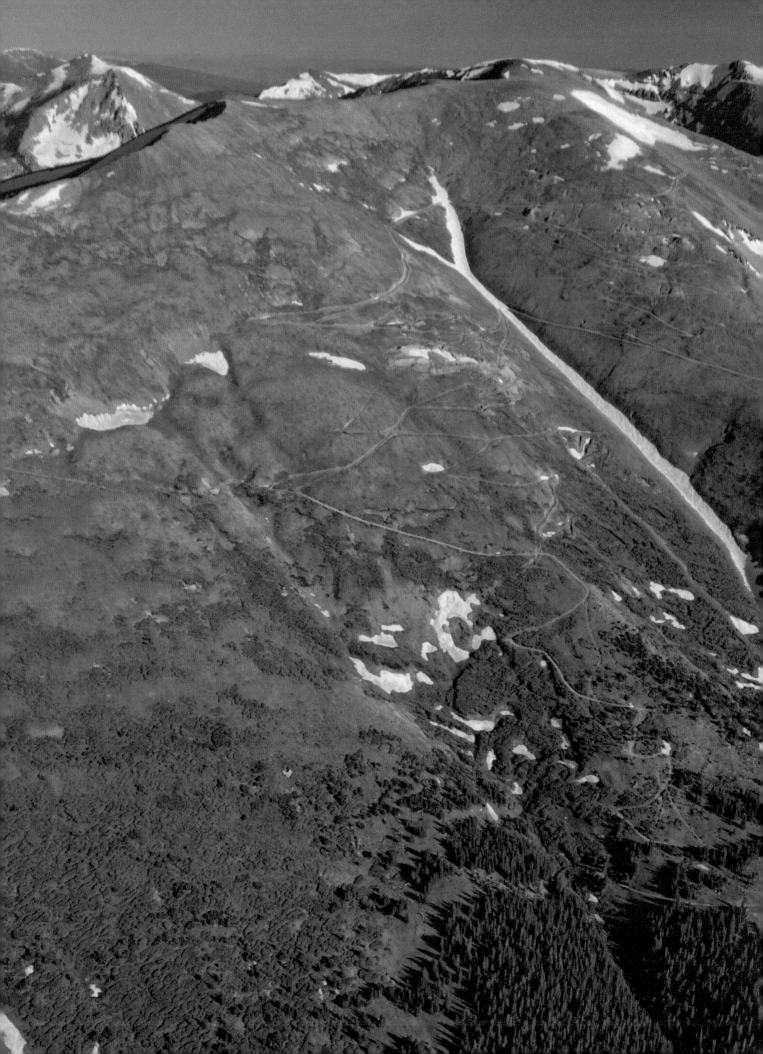

The Mechanics of a 14er

One rule of thumb when comparing a 14er to ordinary terrain is change. Everything about the elevation differences produces a wholesale difference in wind, soil, temperature, moisture, clouds, storms, plants, animals, rocks, and just about anything else a person can think of. As it is, mountain ranges are captivating because of those changes. 14ers in Colorado have just about everything possible, save for tropical plants and extensive glaciers. There is no defined rule as to what to expect at a certain altitude in the state, as all of those thresholds vary, depending on what specific mountain or range we are speaking of. Nine thousand feet might be relatively dry in one place, and extremely snowy with tall trees in another. However, the general rule of what to expect is consistent across the state as one ascends in elevation.

Desert & Sagebrush, Kremmling CO (7,500' to 7,900')

It has long been known that increasing a person's elevation has the equivalent effect of heading closer to the poles. This means that, as one ascends terrain, the weather, plants, and animals that they encounter would be similar to a region quite a distance farther north. A further ascent and the environment changes yet more to something found even farther north than the prior point. This maxim holds true all over the earth, as Canadian spruce forests are found above 6,000 feet in the Southeastern US, and the equivalent of tundra is found at elevations about 4,000 feet in the Northeastern US. These are just a few examples of what happens all over the planet.

Perhaps it is the mechanics of the elevation change that mystifies us. A person can be sipping a latte in Denver with pleasant 75 degree temperatures and blue sky and later that day be merely 40 miles away and 8,000 feet higher and have everything about their surroundings mimic the northernmost regions of Canada. Many visit those sections of Canada; few live there. Perhaps we like to flirt with the uninhabitable, without trying to take it over.

Sagebrush & Cottonwoods, Summit County (8,200')

Whatever our motivations, the environment is predictable. When it comes to moisture, the simple rule is that there is more the higher one goes. It is measured predominately in snow in the Rockies, with tripling and quintupling snowfall quantities at summits compared to valleys. Snow starts in September, though unlikely to stay, and finally melts off in July at these heights. Valleys vary, with the highest inhabited valleys having a snow season of largely October to May, with some variation. The highest average snowfall out of any ski resort is 350" at 12,500 elevation. Fourteeners likely receive closer to 600", though I have no official measurements taken from any peaks. It would be very hard to measure given the wind speeds at the summits.

Temperature obviously declines while elevation increases. Western air loses 5.5 degrees Fahrenheit per 1,000 feet of elevation due to its low relative humidity. Wetter regions have a rate of change closer to 3.3 degrees per 1,000 feet, and that occasionally happens in the summer if things get quite wet. Hence, if temperatures are 50 degrees in Aspen, it would drop to below 20 on the summit of a 14er. That reality accomplishes a number of things. The snow lasts longer due to lower temps, and it affects the ability of things to grow, as the climate is Arctic.

Winds increase ferociously at altitude. There is nothing to stop them, so the jet stream in the upper atmosphere can rage with a fury. While winds can be well in excess of hurricane force, that does not mean that they always are. In the Rockies, my instinct told me the wind would be an unholy fury at all times, and it surprised me how many days it was still. Even more so, I was suprised at how not windy it was at 9,600' in Breckenridge. Granted, weather changes quickly at altitude, and countless lives have been lost due to lack of preparation.

Lodgepole Pine, Breckenridge CO (10,600')

With the backdrop of wind, temperature, and snowfall, it's a matter of putting vegetation in perspective. I will use the elevation levels as the trees were found in Summit County, in the central part of the state, as I lived there for 14 months while getting the photos for the project. It is quite dry up to about 8,000', where sagebrush is common, with aspens in shady sides of terrain, and cottonwoods in creek beds. As the terrain approaches 9,000', lodgepole pine trees are the most common, with groves of aspen mixed in. Steep terrain angled south toward the sun may remain covered in sagebrush. At 10,000', sagebrush is no longer part of the equation, and it is a mix of lodgepole pine, spruce, and some aspen. By 10,750', the aspens are largely gone as are the lodgepole pines, and spruce trees dominate. They increase in stature and height nicely until about 11,300', 200' below timberline, where they get a bit smaller and the timberline rapidly becomes evident, giving way to abundant grass and willow bushes that do not exceed 6 feet in height. Willow bushes last at most to 12,250', where just grass remains. Grasses get thinner and largely disappear around 13,000', and rocks become ever more bleak and pronounced from 13,500' and higher. Many of the summits of higher mountains have little to no soil, merely a pile of rocks jutting into the atmosphere.

Spruce (11,600')

I have given some extensive analysis as to why the trees quit where they do. It is an abrupt transition. One minute you're in the forest, the next wading through grass with incredible views. In the eastern mountains that I had hiked previously, the trees get smaller and smaller – maybe a pine tree is three feet tall with only branches on the leeward side, beat to near death by unrelenting wind, and that tree could be over three hundred years old. Eventually those forsaken trees give way to grass and rock, a timberline forged by storms and unforgiving weather. It doesn't seem that way in the Rockies. It goes from a mature, normal tree to grass, simply and without much fanfare.

Granted, the increase in moisture is healthy for the trees. The higher up, the more groundwater they have to grow, which is the dominant limiting factor in the West at lower altitudes. On the other hand, snow depth increases dramatically, as does avalanche activity. A careful observation of the timberline with relation to the mountains above it will show that it is sliding slabs of snow pummeling down the mountain that wipes the trees out. In fact, the winter of 2013 to 2014 had remarkable snowfall, resulting in some avalanches that came careening down into established forest, taking a sizable chunk out like a bulldozer to matchsticks.

Animals naturally follow vegetation and water; both of those things define their habitat. Mountain goats and bighorn sheep can be found at altitude. I have seen foxes above 12,500', both on foot and from the airplane. There have been accounts of mountain lions traversing ranges with killed prey. Ptarmigans, a type of bird that looks like a pheasant, and marmots, a form of gopher, live above timberline. I have personally seen herds of elk in lodgepole forests at 10,500'. Canada lynx make their habitat somewhere around 11,000', just below timberline. On another occasion, I stumbled across bear caves at 10,750' in thick Engelmann spruce forests. Moose easily make their way from 7,000' to 10,000'. These statements are based on my observation; a thorough study of animal behavior will likely show wider thresholds of permissible habitat. If a person spends a mildly appreciable amount of time in nature in the Rockies, it is a certainty that encounter with animals will be frequented.

Spruce to Grass, Back of Buffalo Mountain (12,400')

There are a few small remaining glaciers in Colorado, found in the Front Range facing northeast. They are nothing appreciable by any standard, not the Alaskan experience with a mighty glacier carving its way to the sea. Old photographs show that these glaciers were more sizable a century ago, not monolithic, though very interesting to see. They are sadly fading with the changes in the atmosphere. Colorado is at the border of an interesting dynamic: a place with the highest peaks in the continental US, a place of extreme conditions and extreme beauty, not yet quite rugged enough to completely deny access. Traveling further south makes the mountains less interesting and foreboding, and traveling north makes them far more hazardous.

Grass to Rock, Peak 1, Frisco CO (12,933')

The wind does move the snow around in interesting ways. A good portion of the year, exposed ridge lines and mountain faces may be relatively free of snow, as the wind scours it off like sandpaper. Such conditions tempt a valley dweller with easy access for off-season hiking, only to be remiss to find out that such snow has to blow somewhere. It finds itself on the leeward side of the mountain – in cornices, bowls, and avalanche traps.

At the end of the analytics behind why the mountains exist as they do, they are an awesome experience, a poetic opportunity to stand in the sky and stare forces that shape our earth in the face. On one hand, we are reminded of the limitations of human reach, and on another, we are able to experience something that instincts tell us we cannot.

Front Range

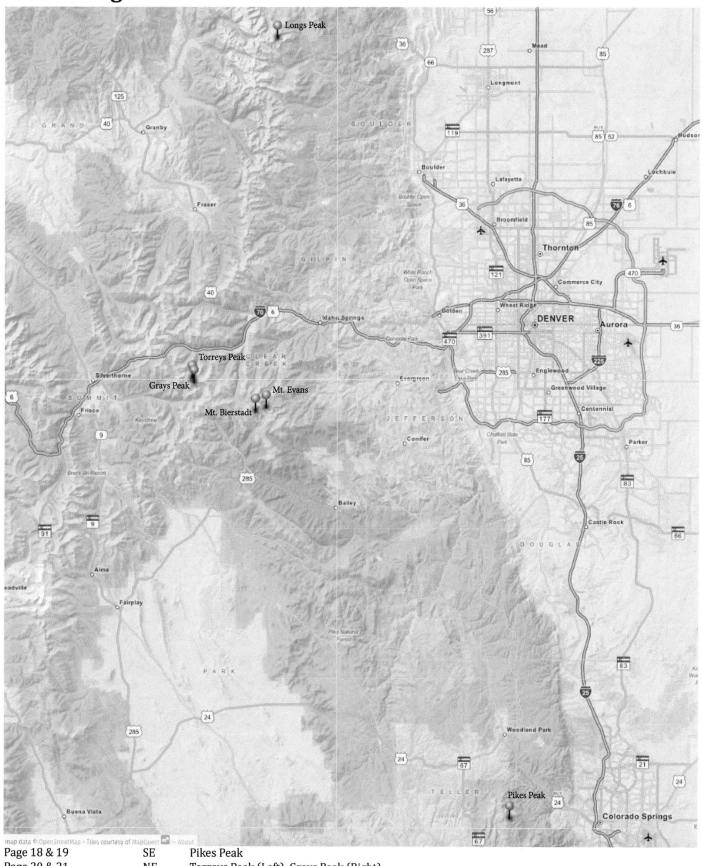

Page 18 & 19	SE	Pikes Peak
Page 20 & 21	NE	Torreys Peak (Left), Grays Peak (Right)
Page 22 & 23	E	Longs Peak
Page 24 & 25	E	Mt. Evans (Center Left), Mt. Bierstadt (Right)
Page 26 (Top)	E	Mt. Evans (Center Left), Mt. Bierstadt (Right)
Page 26 (Middle)	W	Mt. Evans (Summit), Mt. Bierstadt (Rear)
Page 26 (Bottom)	NW	Mt. Evans (Summit)

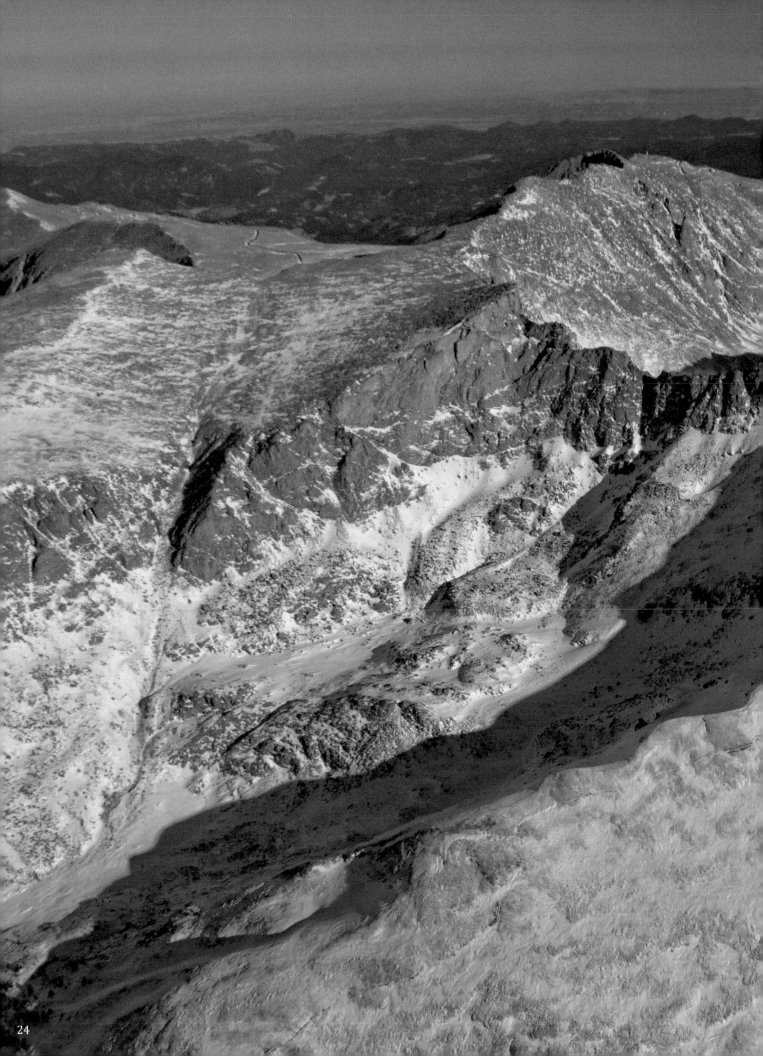

Front Range

The Front Range is as quintessential as it gets. When millions of residents living on the western edge of the Great Plains drive to work, get a latte, pump gasoline, or buy groceries, they are constantly looking at these sentinels of wilderness, mountains peering down on an urban area and presenting a reminder that harshness and the great wild lies within miles of modern, urban living. Visitors that come to the urban corridor for non-wilderness experiences tell lively tales of the mountains visible from the city, an anomaly in American life that sticks in the minds of visitors. It is these particular 14ers that people are talking about.

Mt. Bierstadt (Right), Mt. Evans (Center Left), Looking East

Geologically speaking, they aren't very organized. The other ranges in the Rockies have consistent ridgelines or groupings of peaks, where the proximity of one 14er to another makes some form of logical sense. While not a geologist, I must say that the Front Range appears to be organized more by common view than analysis of rock stratiforms.

Mt. Evans Summit, Mt. Bierstadt in Rear

From an aviation perspective, the Front Range has the most severe winds out of all of the ranges, with downdrafts that can smash an airliner into the ground. For all of you nervous airline passengers, commercial flights stay far enough away from the ridgelines to avoid those winds. Nonetheless, were a 737 to fly along my Piper Cub near the summits, it could, much like me, get smashed out of the sky with the meteorological fly swatter. It is also the range that hosts the two most isolated 14ers: Longs Peak in Rocky Mountain National Park and Pikes Peak near Colorado Springs. Both of these peaks required flight over silly terrain to get to, as much effort as some ranges with ten 14ers, yet the reward was a photo over one mountain. It would be accurate to create a "risk of death ratio" and label the per capita risk of death ratio as being highest for these two, given the effort required.

Mt. Evans, one of the 14ers that I drove to the top of (Pikes Peak is the other drivable 14er), has the dubious distinction of being the peak where I came very close to being struck by lightning. It was June 30, and what appeared to be a snow shower was approaching. Thunderstorms were moving away from Denver, with some distant rumbles that could be heard. Due to the dryness of the atmosphere, lightning is far more prevalent with smaller storms in the West; hence, some describe it as apocalyptic. Nonetheless, I was about to climb the final four-foot rock to stand on the pinnacle of Mt. Evans. Some clueless souls offered to take my picture. As I stood there (a misstep would have resulted in a 1,500' fall to certain death), I noticed that something didn't seem exactly right and commented: "You might want to hurry up. I am the highest lightning rod in the eastern half of the state." At that moment, I heard a zapping sound, followed by a sharp pain and the feeling of electricity in my right calf and simultaneous electrical flow on the top of my skull. I yelled: "There's static!" and the 20 people on the summit scattered like a mouse beneath a hawk, a veritable "poof" and ensuing dust cloud and they were gone. My response was to launch into the air, descend 4 feet to the next wet rock, and scamper down with a remarkable haste, hiding beneath a rock outcropping until my camera came down with the slothful and ignorant folks who never did take a picture of my near death experience. It was not a lightning strike, rather a static buildup that meant that a strike was quite imminent. My leg swelled some over the remainder of the day, and the experience turned out to be the beginning of a summer of near-death experiences, one of the many benefits of life in Summit County, CO.

Mt. Evans Summit, Don't Fall

Elk Mountains

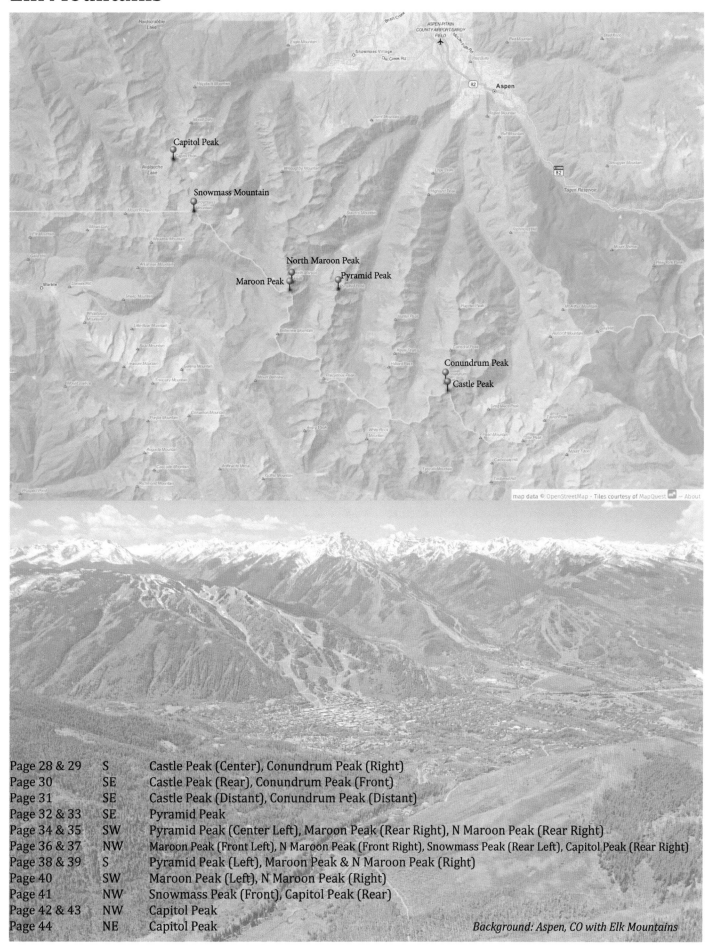

Page 28 & 29	S	Castle Peak (Center), Conundrum Peak (Right)
Page 30	SE	Castle Peak (Rear), Conundrum Peak (Front)
Page 31	SE	Castle Peak (Distant), Conundrum Peak (Distant)
Page 32 & 33	SE	Pyramid Peak
Page 34 & 35	SW	Pyramid Peak (Center Left), Maroon Peak (Rear Right), N Maroon Peak (Rear Right)
Page 36 & 37	NW	Maroon Peak (Front Left), N Maroon Peak (Front Right), Snowmass Peak (Rear Left), Capitol Peak (Rear Right)
Page 38 & 39	S	Pyramid Peak (Left), Maroon Peak & N Maroon Peak (Right)
Page 40	SW	Maroon Peak (Left), N Maroon Peak (Right)
Page 41	NW	Snowmass Peak (Front), Capitol Peak (Rear)
Page 42 & 43	NW	Capitol Peak
Page 44	NE	Capitol Peak

Background: Aspen, CO with Elk Mountains

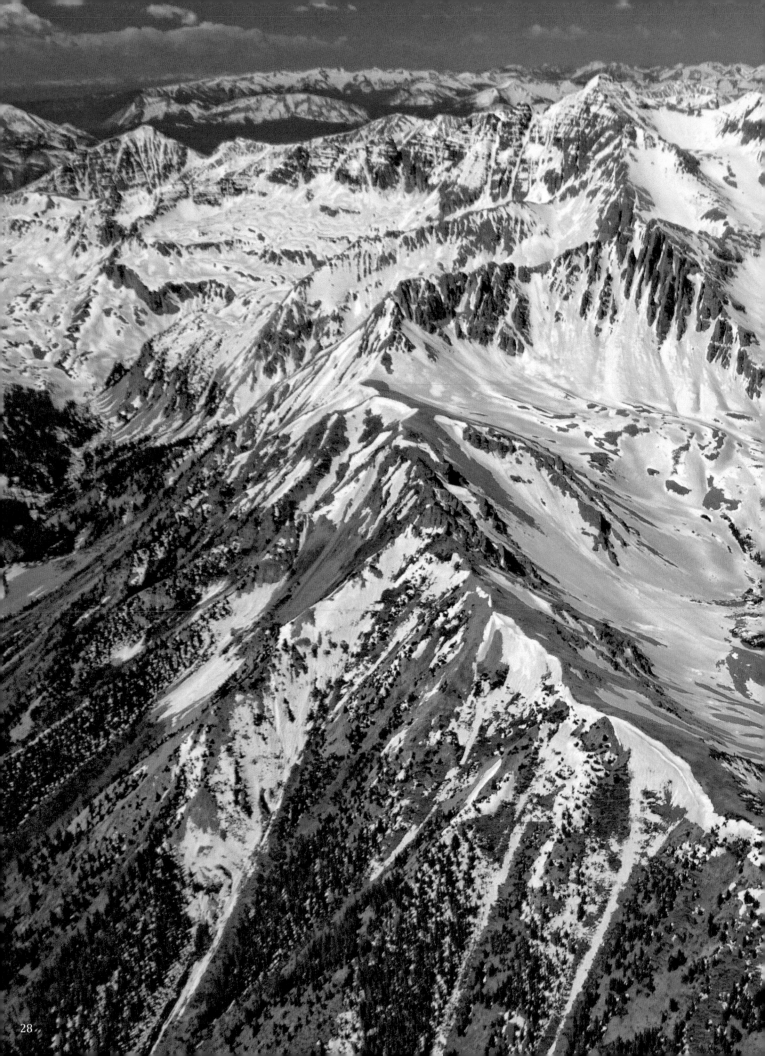

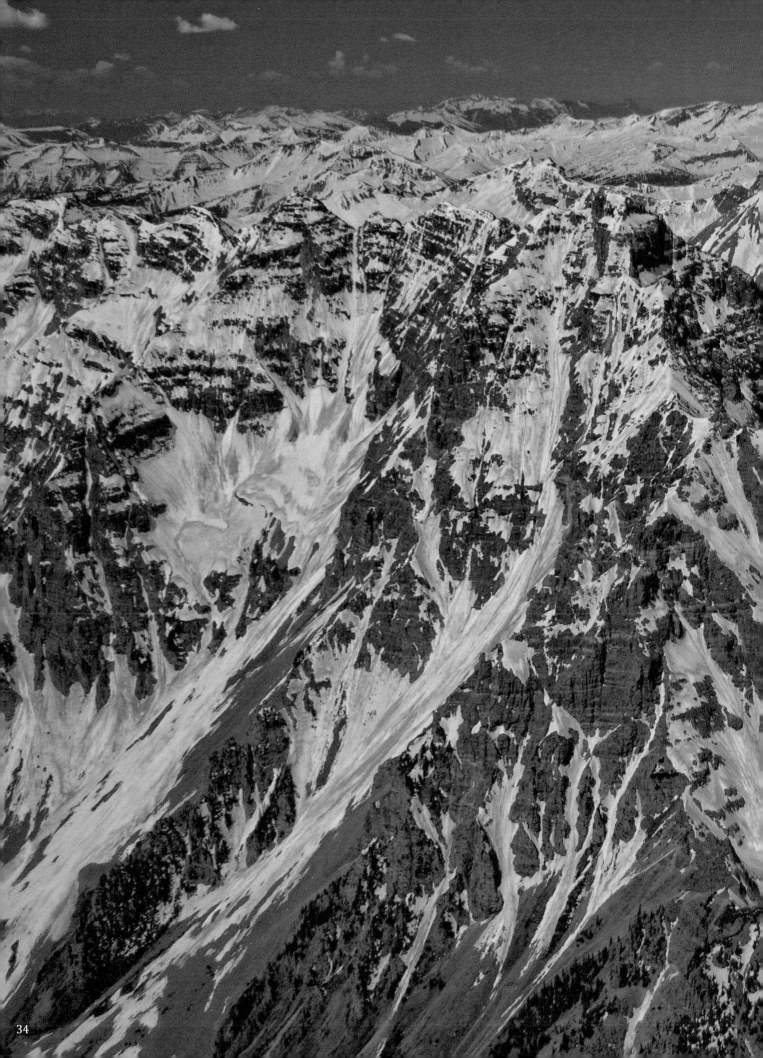

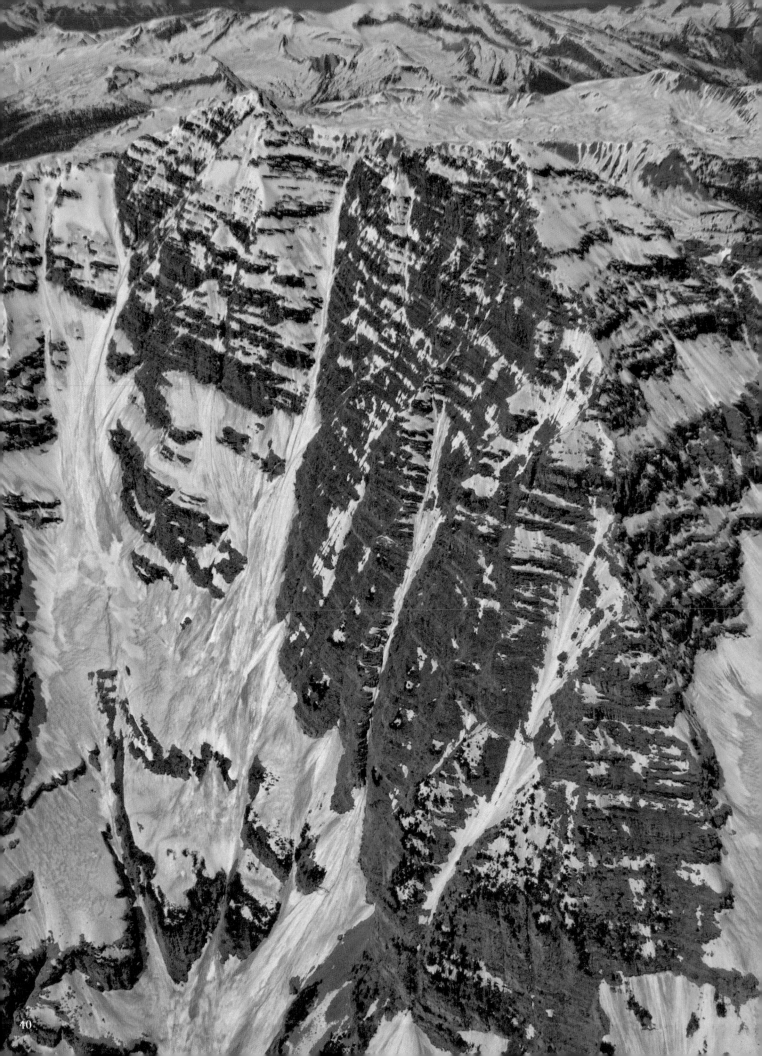

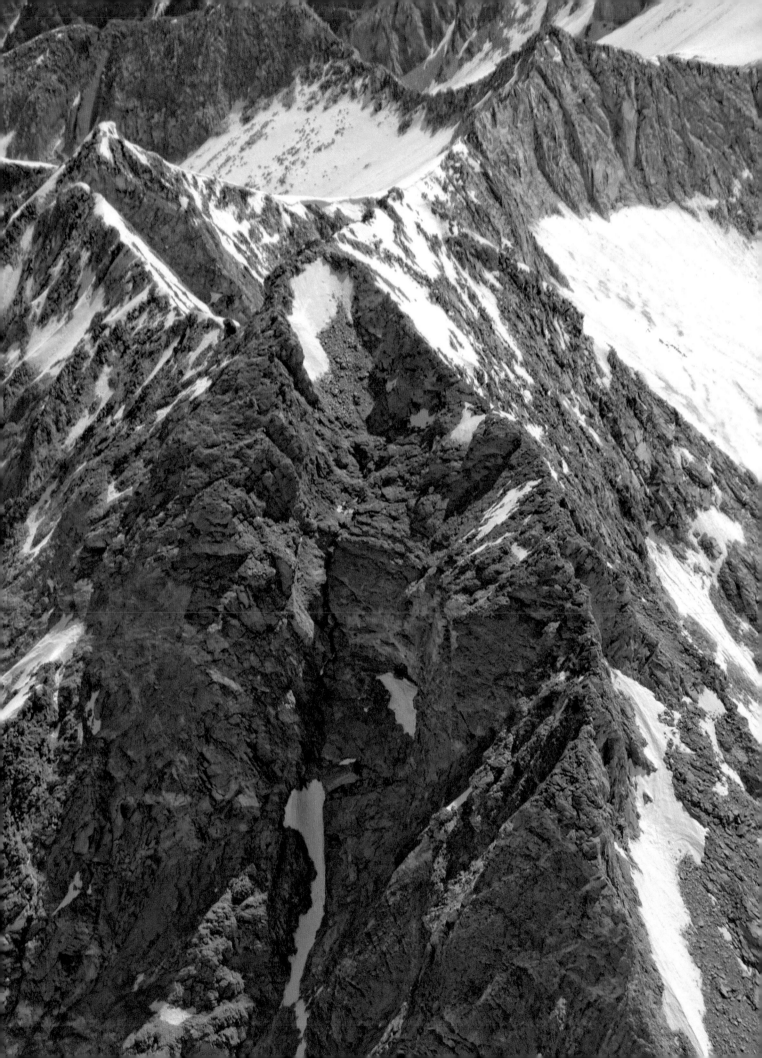

Flying in the Rocky Mountains

For non-pilots, most people get highly neurotic when the subject becomes about an airplane. Pilots tend to roll their eyes and think that the general population is a bunch of ignorant sissies, and then go on to relate embellished and exaggerated stories of danger and adventure, merely perpetuating the cycle for fun. When it comes to mountain flying, and especially high-altitude mountain flying, suddenly pilots turn into big sissies, though they will hide it at a cocktail party.

High altitude flying, by itself, doesn't spook pilots too much. The dangers are weather and less oxygen, the lack of oxygen being the culprit that leads to confusion, euphoria, and stupid decision-making. There are hypothermia risks, and higher speed traffic. In a non-mountain environment where a pilot chooses to fly at high altitude, he or she is pretty much in control of the situation, and can descend to deal with hypoxia, cold, or weather concerns.

Mountain flying scares most pilots. Even the low-altitude Appalachians in the East Coast can produce rotors and downdrafts. Downdrafts are obvious, wind coming down the side of the mountain and smashing airplanes like pancakes into the ground. Rotors are insidious. As wind ascends a peak and continues

Gore Range with Approaching Thunderstorm

ascending long after having reached the top of the mountain, a rotating tube of air develops on the lee side. It is stationary and sits there spinning so long as the wind is blowing perpendicular to the mountain range. On one side of the rotor, an airplane is involuntarily pushed upward, sometimes with power at idle. Likewise, the opposing side of the rotor involuntarily pushes the airplane downward, even at full power. These phenomena are dangerous if a pilot is vulnerable and the situation presents itself at the wrong time.

Couple high altitude and mountain flying together, and pilots lose the bravado and are suddenly made aware of their mortality. There is another component of high altitude flying that is not a problem in wide-open skies. When coupled with terrain, it can quickly become deadly. Everything about an airplane performs with a grand sluggishness at high altitude. The propeller grabs less air. The engine has less air to intake; therefore, horsepower decreases. The design of the wing requires the same air density, measured in sea level altitude, to perform. Therefore, everything happens faster: stall speeds, takeoff speeds, landing speeds. Descents are quicker (akin to a rock off a bridge, if high enough), takeoffs and climbs are sluggish. Now combine all of that with terrain and the weather associated with terrain: downdrafts, rotors, and the like. It is a lethal combination for the uninformed and the panicky.

Some of the issues in Colorado are very real. Certain general aviation aircraft models can barely climb above 12,000 feet, and a number of air routes need 13,000' or more to safely traverse mountain ranges. In that case, it is not an option. In other cases, some aircraft that do go through can barely handle it. Add one factor of unpredictability and things can get quite dangerous. With danger present, panic is the nail in the coffin, obfuscating clear thinking and decision making, resulting in a death that often is quite avoidable.

As if all of that is not enough, pilots have stark consequences staring them in the face. Each vertical mountainside is a cliff that might mean their demise. Beneath each flight of mystical fancy is a potential gravesite in the event of engine failure. Being that the terrain is either in the woods, above the rocky timberline, or in deep snow, an emergency landing that doesn't injure or kill the pilot or passengers could result in death if survival is not handled properly. Although aircraft are equipped with an emergency locator transmitter that activates upon impact, the average time until rescue is measured in many hours, as the signal has to be received, confirmed, transmitted to the right agencies, a plan coordinated, and then executed. If the weather goes sour in this process, it may be days before help arrives.

Drama aside, there are ways to handle flying in the mountains safely. Altitude is the friend of any pilot around mountains; hence, anytime a larger buffer between the airplane and ground is possible, that is a good thing. This would especially be the case with certain passes that have mountains towering on either side. Altitude is stored energy, which can be used to get a plane out of a

Too Windy for Flying, Breckenridge CO

rotor or downdraft. It also is more likely to keep the airplane out of the downdraft or rotor to begin with, as the farther from the peaks, the farther from the weather associated with them. Think of a long-distance flight in an airliner over mountains, 20,000' above them – it is an uneventful occurrence. Putting that same airliner flying between towering peaks would be terrifying.

Planning is another component. Upper level wind forecasts are very accurate, so a pilot can get anticipated wind speed and direction at a host of altitudes. Twenty knot wind speeds or less is generally safe, with a buffer to 30 knots having been just fine in my airplane. The Colorado Rockies is not the place to play with low clouds and marginal situations – as simply flying up there is quite marginal as it is.

Learning to fly like a glider pilot is a highly useful skill. While I do not have my glider certificate, I had to learn what gliders know about thermals and updrafts. Without an updraft, climbing takes quite a long time in my aircraft, and finding updrafts was a way

Poor Example of Terrain Clearance

to save time and money. In some instances, it meant the difference between getting over a mountain range or not. Knowledge of updraft locations also means knowledge of downdrafts. What goes up correspondingly will go down, so knowing at least one of those pieces of the puzzle usually leaves a spot to fit the left over piece. Updrafts can be quite strong, providing an elevator to the sky if timed properly.

Stupidity is best to be avoided. The best advice I got was to "know how to get out of a situation before you go into it" and "don't go somewhere where you're stuck if the winds turn." The only way I have gotten up close and personal with a mountain peak is if I have figured out the wind conditions, am informed with weather reports, and after having some experience. A rule of thumb that I have determined is to never approach a mountain from an altitude below the summit if a crossing is being attempted. Unless the aircraft is a rocket, getting into a low airspeed situation, hoping to be able to climb over the summit in time is deadly. Many accidents resulting in fatalities involve an attempt to out climb terrain with an underperforming airplane. Far too late, a turn is attempted and, at low airspeeds, the airplane stalls and heads into the ground. Adding 1,000 feet of altitude would obviate the entire disaster.

Getting Close to Mt. Sopris

At the conclusion of quite a long time flying in some fairly crazy terrain, experience and training is the best safety margin. Everything about flying in high terrain can be mitigated, so long as the pilot understands what the danger is and what the compensatory action is. While it seems pretty simple to suggest that more pilots know what they are doing, I have to realize that the practicality of flying in such terrain is fairly low. Pilots are taught to and spend most of their time avoiding the highest peaks altogether, effectively becoming their servant. While that is wise in some respects, there is an opportunity lost to become the master of these summits, increasing safety overall and being able to enjoy an unforgettable experience.

Author's Antique Airplane: Piper PA-11 on a fuel stop at Telluride, CO Airport

Flying in the Rockies is not for the faint of heart or the uninformed. Much like driving, skiing, hiking, or climbing in the Rockies, everything about the experience requires more planning, knowledge, and prevention – as the situation is marginal across the board. More weather issues can happen, cell reception is less, and situations quickly get bad in the event of injury in the wilderness. It is the same with an airplane and, like the hundreds of thousands of visitors to Colorado on the ground that enjoy an injury-free excursion, the vast majority of flights don't end in a smoldering crater.

Sawatch Range

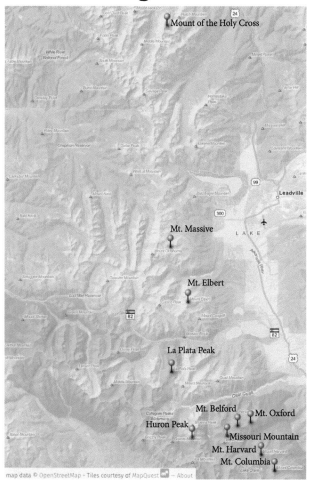

Northern Sawatch Range

Southern Sawatch Range

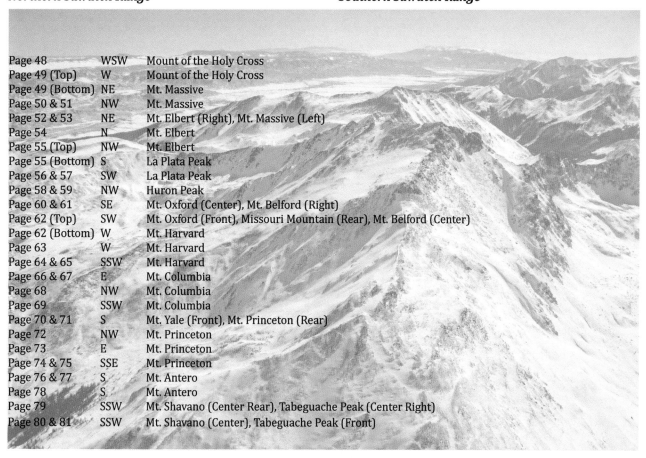

Page 48	WSW	Mount of the Holy Cross
Page 49 (Top)	W	Mount of the Holy Cross
Page 49 (Bottom)	NE	Mt. Massive
Page 50 & 51	NW	Mt. Massive
Page 52 & 53	NE	Mt. Elbert (Right), Mt. Massive (Left)
Page 54	N	Mt. Elbert
Page 55 (Top)	NW	Mt. Elbert
Page 55 (Bottom)	S	La Plata Peak
Page 56 & 57	SW	La Plata Peak
Page 58 & 59	NW	Huron Peak
Page 60 & 61	SE	Mt. Oxford (Center), Mt. Belford (Right)
Page 62 (Top)	SW	Mt. Oxford (Front), Missouri Mountain (Rear), Mt. Belford (Center)
Page 62 (Bottom)	W	Mt. Harvard
Page 63	W	Mt. Harvard
Page 64 & 65	SSW	Mt. Harvard
Page 66 & 67	E	Mt. Columbia
Page 68	NW	Mt. Columbia
Page 69	SSW	Mt. Columbia
Page 70 & 71	S	Mt. Yale (Front), Mt. Princeton (Rear)
Page 72	NW	Mt. Princeton
Page 73	E	Mt. Princeton
Page 74 & 75	SSE	Mt. Princeton
Page 76 & 77	S	Mt. Antero
Page 78	S	Mt. Antero
Page 79	SSW	Mt. Shavano (Center Rear), Tabeguache Peak (Center Right)
Page 80 & 81	SSW	Mt. Shavano (Center), Tabeguache Peak (Front)

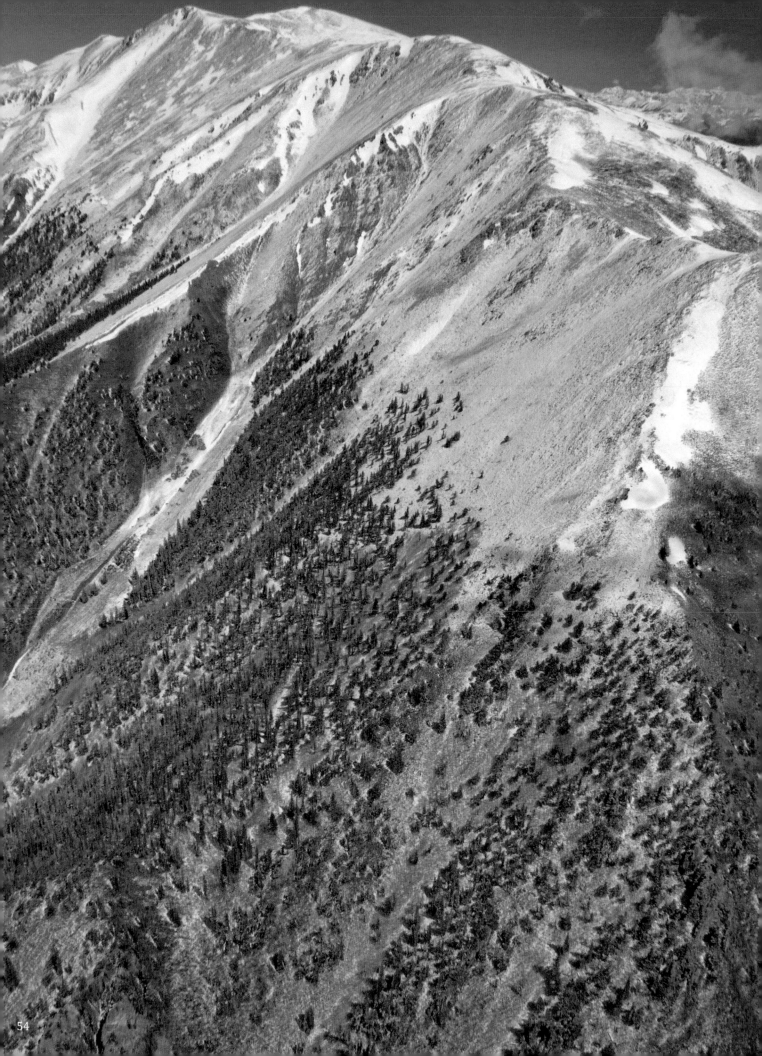

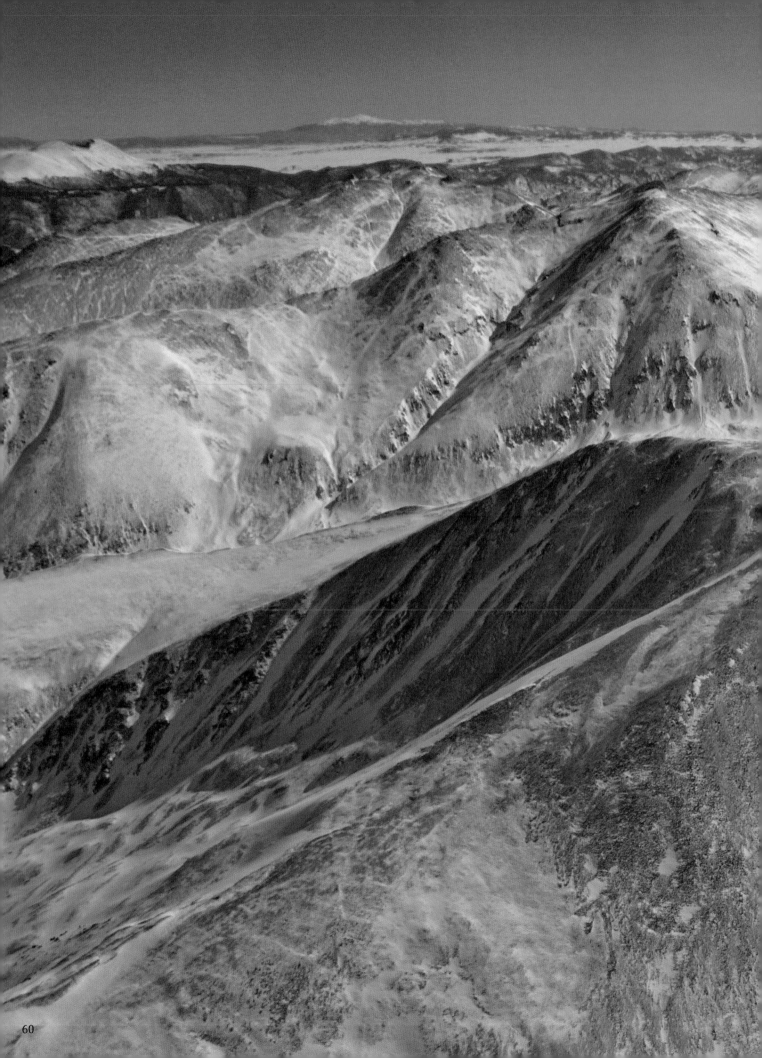

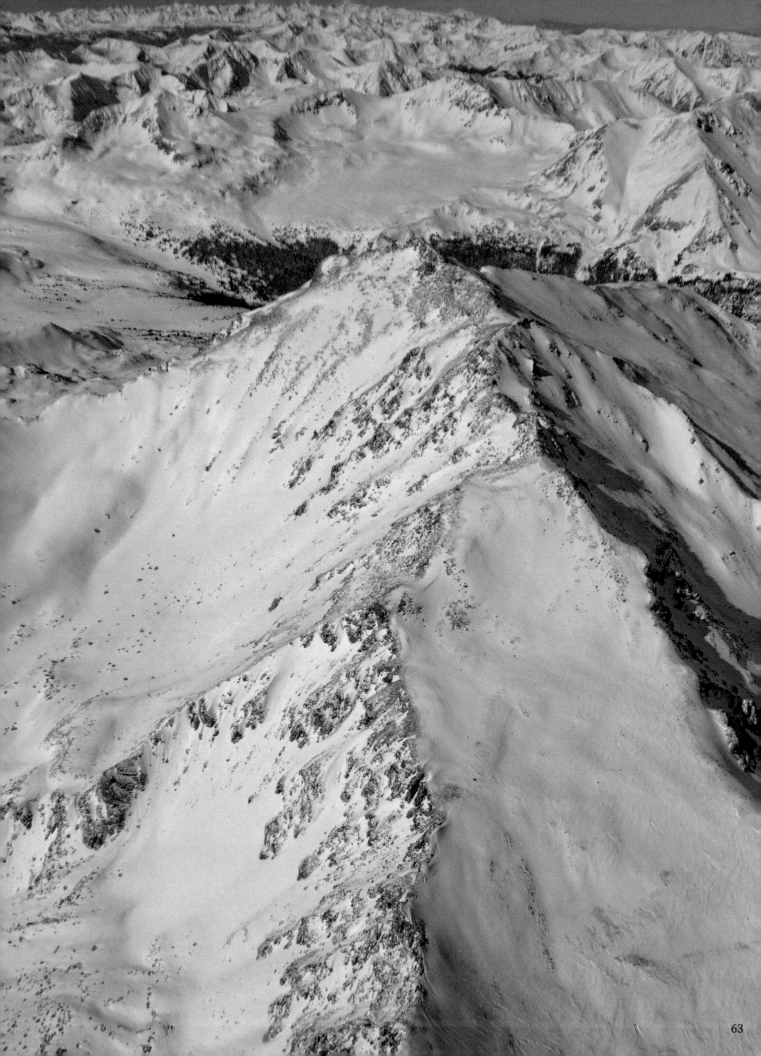

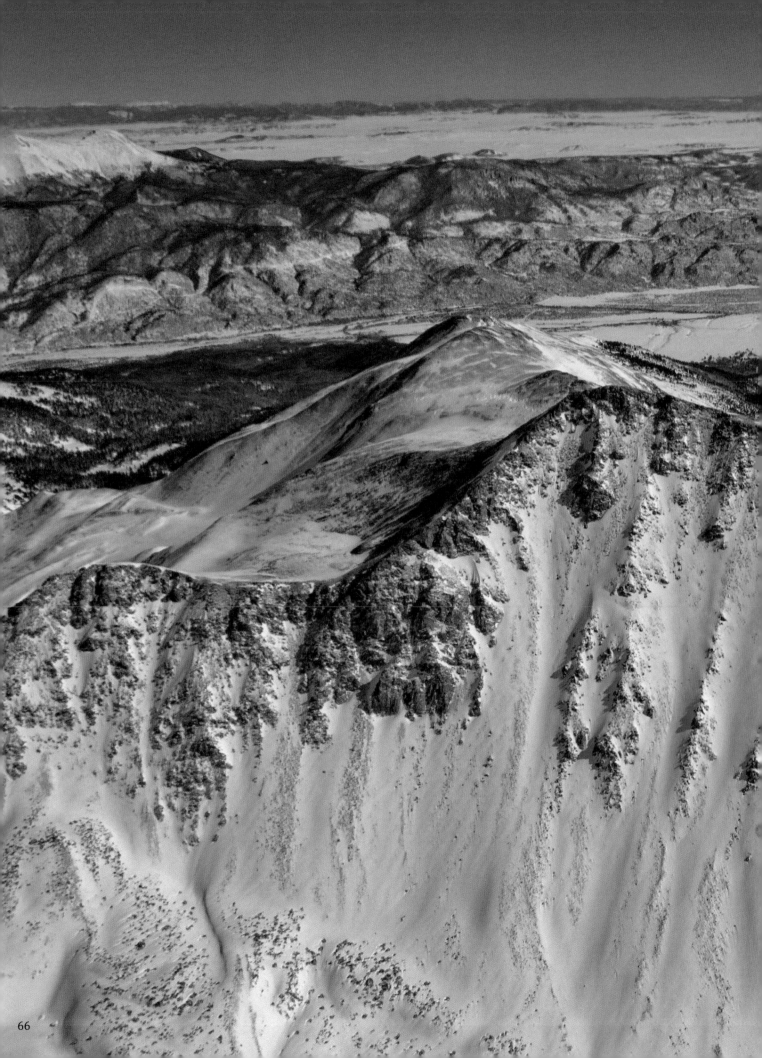

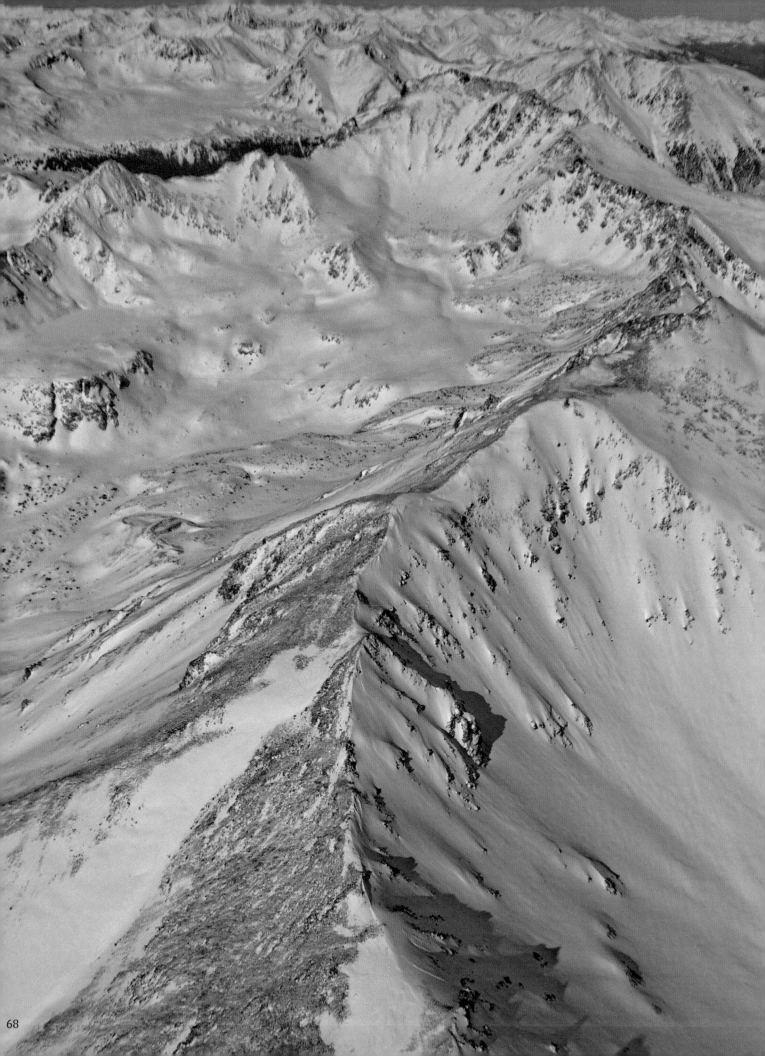

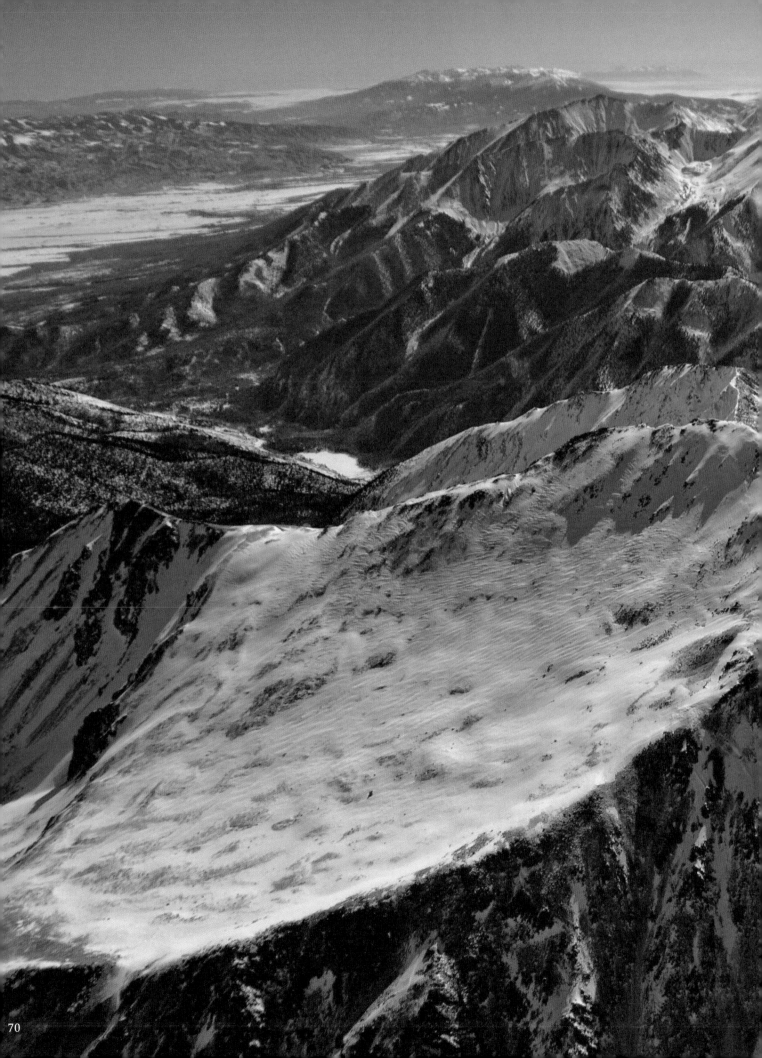

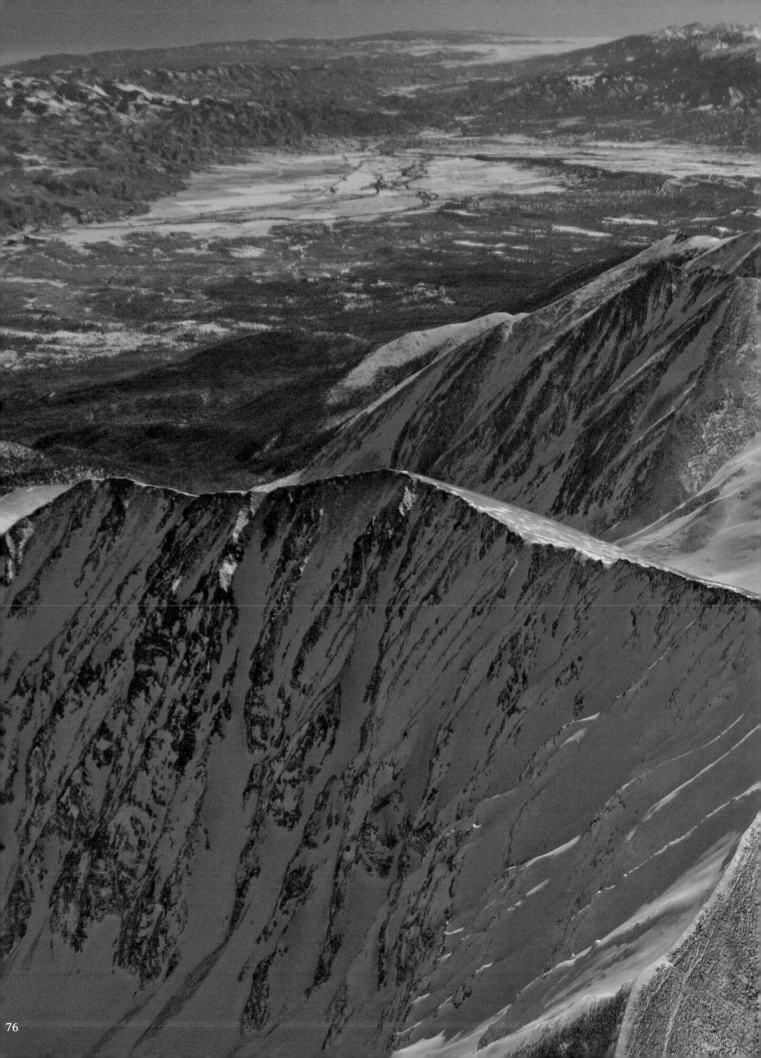

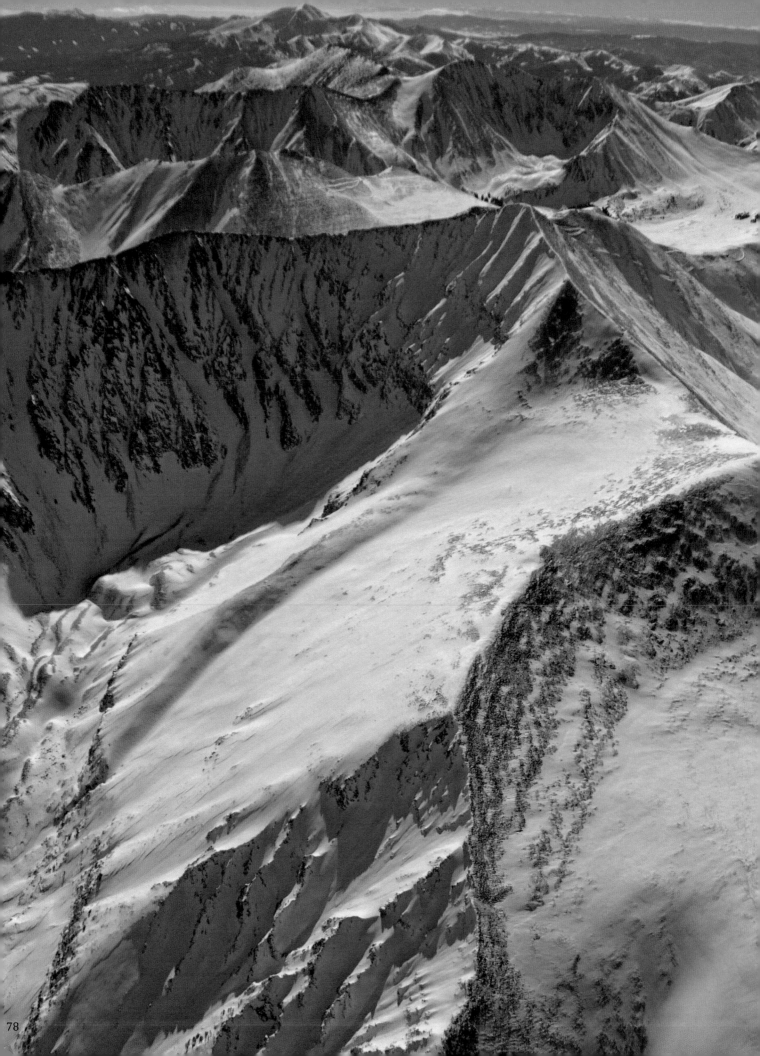

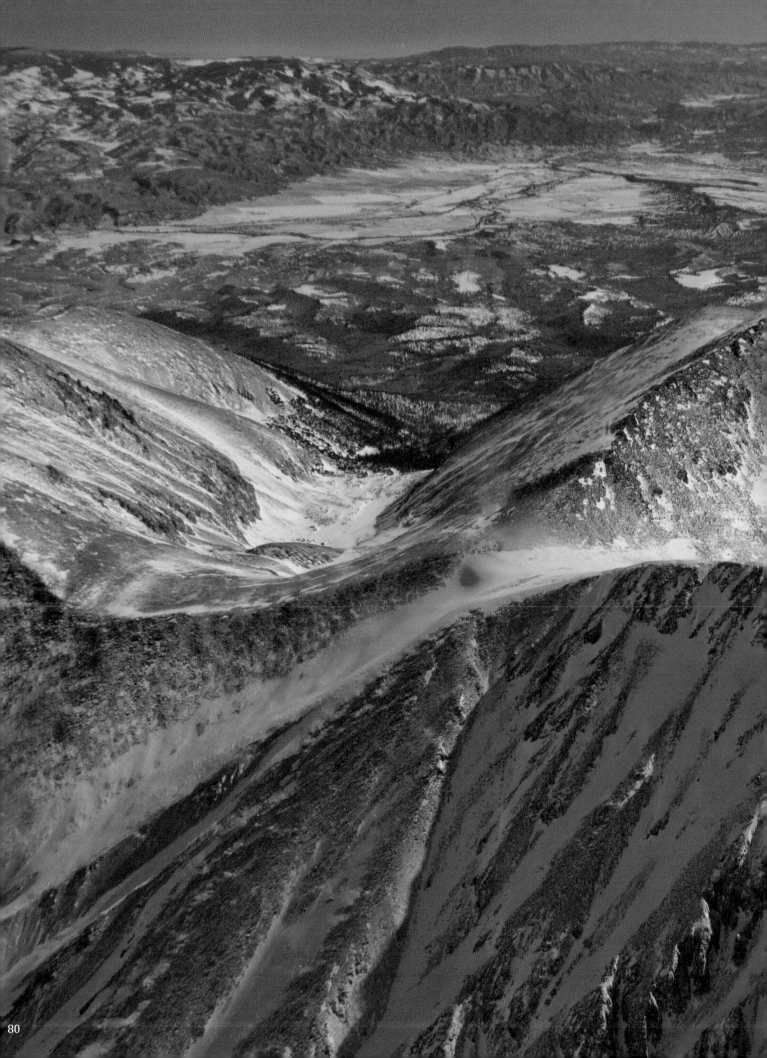

My Mountain Flying Experience

It all begins in 2010, when I took my first flight into mountainous terrain. A new client situation in West Virginia materialized, so I took the flight from Charlotte, NC in a rented Cessna 152. My previously longest flight was 75 miles, and this had been over 10 years prior. While I had gotten current with a couple of lessons, I had effectively flown 5 times in the entire decade. I was rusty and eager for adventure, a gloriously lethal combination.

It had snowed all over the southeast, and it was cold. There was no GPS, merely a map and VOR navigation, which is ground-based navigation using 1960s-era radio signals. The flight would be 150 miles over the Appalachians in NC, VA, and into WV. I got the airplane started despite the cold, went through the exhaustive checklists and was ready to taxi. Adding power, I went nowhere. More power….and I looked down to see the wheel chocks were still in. Power down, take them out, power up. I was nervous and it was showing. I finally took off with great anticipation, tracking my pencil line I had drawn onto the map as I headed north into the higher terrain.

It was breezy at both surface airports. That meant that the winds were going pretty good at altitude. I knew that rotors were the tools of the devil, invisible beasts that lurk in the Appalachians and swallow airplanes. So, just to be safe, I flew a mile above the terrain. That is correct, I had 5,000 feet of terrain clearance. Ironically, the rotors were still going up there – strong up and downdrafts – oscillating just like I had read in the aviation magazines.

Map-based navigation seemed to be fine, though I did configure the VOR to cross check, just in case. Visibility was over 100 miles – clear March 6 air – with snow all over the mountains and valleys. It was a beautiful sight, though I feared the landing. What kind of turbulence would be over the mountains? Would it break the airplane in half?

Aviation Mountain Virginity Lost, Wytheville VA

Sure enough, the final ridge near the airport banged the plane around good. Winds were quite erratic and strong and the surface, and I managed to do a landing that I at least wasn't ashamed of. After concluding my business for the day, I flew back with a giant smile on my face. Upon landing, my instructor asked, "Where did you go on a day like this?" "West Virginia." "Did you have a GPS?" "No." "Oh my god…" I thought he was being dramatic, though I am a nut for maps.

NY to NC Flight, Highest Terrain, Virginia

I made the same flight about 8 times over the next 4 months, with all sorts of weather: thunderstorms, low clouds, fog issues, and the like. My confidence grew with each trip, and I began to fear the mountains less and less, traversing them with 1,500' to 2,000' clearance instead of a mile. My grandfather did not like the concept one bit, and made his thoughts known constantly, suggesting that I just "forget those mountains."

Later in 2010, I took possession of the PA-11 that I now fly. That required a flight from Buffalo, NY to Charlotte, NC. I was content to make the flight in October. My grandfather suggested disassembling the aircraft and driving it down, for which I couldn't understand the purpose of aviation at that point. Other family members tried to impose various edicts and rules. They finally collectively got their nerves in order when I agreed to take my grandfather's GPS and file a flight plan, the latter of which proved to cause more problems than solve. The tallest mountain I crossed was no higher than 3,000 feet above sea level. It was uneventful, and as of then my longest trip at 500 miles.

I did some flying in the NC Mountains, though not too frequently, even though they are the tallest in the eastern part of the US. I had one notable incident over Lake Lure, NC, at 3,000' altitude, where downdrafts in a snow shower were so strong that the airplane was slowly losing altitude at full power. I was in a canyon and pulled what is effectively an aerobatic maneuver, a wingover, to turn 180 degrees without smashing into the canyon side. Between that and the rotors from some years prior, what the magazines wrote about was real. It is ironic that the downdraft on that day in NC would exceed anything I got myself into in CO.

The next flirtation with mountains was the flight from NC to CO. On my third day of flying, I was crossing the forlorn and desolate sections of western Kansas and eastern Colorado. These are plains of such dryness and desolation that it is hard to describe, grasslands of the harshest aspect, bordering on desert. It is windswept, baked land of tornados and blizzards, a crucible of humanity. With temperatures well over 100 degrees, engine oil at 210 degrees, and engine heat blowing into the cockpit, it was everything not to pass out when I got to Boulder. Ground temps were 96 degrees at 5,300' elevation, with a looming thunderstorm at the Continental Divide. At the advice of the airport manager, I opted to come back and get the airplane another day.

Weeks later, that day came amidst a rather busy Colorado monsoon season. I would be crossing at Rollins Pass, an elevation of less than 12,000'. I had previously taken the PA-11 in the 1990s up to 14,000' in NY, an experience of remarkable sluggishness.

Entering Rockies for First Time, Rollins Pass, CO

I knew it could be done and it had to be done to get it to its new home airport in Kremmling. As I powered up on takeoff in Boulder, the engine started coughing and sputtering just after I got airborne, usually not a good outcome. Seeing as it had never done such a thing, I figured altitude was to blame and tried adjusting the carburetor fuel mixture from full rich to a leaner setting. The coughing stopped and the engine dragged its way into a slow climb. This was the first time I had ever adjusted mixture on takeoff.

As I climbed into the foothills at 8,000', the view was remarkable, though the climb was sluggish. I found that the thermals were very strong vertically, both up and down, and I found upward air currents anywhere a cumulus cloud sat over a hill. Thus, I circled my way up following the clouds and the hawks. At 10,500', the airplane wouldn't climb or put out a reasonable RPM. With my newfound lesson on takeoff, I tried aggressive mixture adjustments and was shocked to see the engine offer 2400 RPM, very close to full RPM (not quite full HP due to altitude). Sluggishly, we made our way to 13,000' as I got closer to the Divide. The terrain was stunning, an alpine cornucopia of incredible scenery, eye candy of a magnitude that cannot be appreciated from the ground.

As I approached the pass, my concern was emergency landing locations. It was evident the timberline was gentle and grassy, with loads of 4x4 vehicles offroading. I would be in good company if I had to land. My next concern was the cloud deck that was pressing in over the pass. Being that I was about to enter the lion's mouth, my concern was clouds that would swoop down and instantly envelop my flight path, an intentional act of malicious sky spirits.

It was uneventful. I flew over the pass. No bumps. No downdrafts. No Satan-induced cloud problems. The other side was sunny, and the terrain dropped below, making it seem awkward that I would remain 6,000' above the ground. Although "in the mountains," it seemed more like rolling hill country in Grand County than a sawtooth death trap of orography. The demons with pitch-forks I had imagined were not, in fact, lurking behind granite spires of death. There were no alligators, nor were there piles of plane wrecks with rotting pilot corpses. It was a pleasant summer day in the high country. I had a feeling of accomplishment as well as the nagging suspicion that I was a drama queen. Maybe mountains aren't so bad.

Peak 1 En Route to Leadville, Frisco CO

As the wife had quite a drive from Boulder to Kremmling, I decided to fly around for fun. I am used to the quintessential Piper Cub experience, flying with the door open at low cruise RPM. That was not happening at 9,000' with sunbaked terrain. I needed 30% more power to fly, and it was an alternation between rising air and descending air. One could not rest flying up here, it was a constant exercise tracking what the wind was doing vertically. After many hours of practice over several months, I finally fell into a routine where flying got fun and easy at the same time.

Four months later, the airplane would move to its most amazing home to date: Leadville CO, the highest airport in North America with a field elevation of 9,927'. The flight over was lots of fun, wedging between mountain peaks and snow showers, over passes,

Leadville Airport with Mt. Sherman (14,035')

under tight clouds, and into the valley. When I got there, the wind was blowing around in swirls, with all three airport windsocks blowing in different directions. I managed to land like I was flying a refrigerator, a distinctly different experience at 10,000' compared to sea level. After some practice rounds, the folks at the airport advised that, absent flying during a snow storm or howling wind, this is as bad as a flyable day gets.

The thing about Leadville is that it is surrounded by peaks over 14,000', all visible from the hangar. A pilot with the slightest shred of adventure will take very little time before desiring to find out what flying over there is like. The airplane arrived in late October to Leadville and the 14ers project started in mid-November. You can see how long the connection took to fire in my mind. From "hmmm…. I wonder about those mountains" to a full-fledged book in a remarkably short period of time.

The actual flying to get the photos was a progressive process of experience and getting comfortable with what I was doing. I first elected to photograph the 14ers of the Mosquito Range, between Leadville airport and Brecken-ridge. I chose those mountains as I was most familiar with them from the ground. Initially quite nervous, I kept my distance and the photos I acquired that day did not make it into the book, as they weren't all that dynamic. After that flight, I photographed the two most looming peaks from the airport: Mt. Elbert and Mt. Massive. This was the first flight where I got close enough that the photos were worth publishing.

Highest Peaks in CO, A Few Miles West of Airport

The floodgates opened at that point. The following flight featured calm upper level winds, so I went up to Mount of the Holy Cross as well as some of the Mosquito Range again. This flight was quite a blast, as I carved around peaks in the Tenmile Range and got quite up close and personal.

Next up was a somewhat breezy day, where I did the peaks in the mid Front Range as well as Pike's Peak. The first clue that the engine was getting erratic on me was while between Grays and Torreys Peak, when the winds shifted from accelerating the aircraft to putting the engine under load. It sputtered some, and was resolved with a mixture change. I thought nothing of it, only had to get my nerves back where they belong.

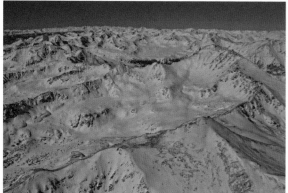

Too Risky - Collegiate Peaks and Elk Mountains

The next flight was the best out of all of them. I had intended to go to the area south of Aspen and photograph the 14ers in the Elk Mountains. As I ascended over Twin Lakes in the Collegiate Range, all I saw was an endless sea of peaks stretching to the horizon. While an awesome sight, it was also minus 5 degrees Fahrenheit when I took off at 10,000' and these ranges had just received over three feet of snow. An engine failure would likely mean death, so I opted to photograph the Collegiate Peaks in the Sawatch Range. An engine out there would be a pleasant glide to the inhabited valley beneath, so I was far more comfortable with the idea.

The visibility was incredible, and the peaks were almost crystalized in their visual purity. The photographs were amazing, so beautiful that I was not noticing that I was utterly freezing. Minus 5 at the ground means something like minus 20 at altitude. While the aircraft has "heat," it does not function at such low exterior temperatures; hence, I was in double ski gear and carried a load of survival equipment. In order to get clear photographs, I have to open the window, offering a blast of 85mph wind in the cockpit. It certainly was unimaginably cold; yet, for those that know me, when I am in pursuit of something, I am not to be stopped. A little chilly air would not be interrupting this trip!

Visibility was at least 100 miles. It was the clearest air I had ever flown in, a blue sky so clear and iridescent that it could be put in a bottle and drank. As I got to the southern reaches of the Sawatch Range, I could see the Sangre de Cristo Range in its glorious splendor, with the next 14ers being about 50 miles away. Although I did not have my 14ers map printed out for these reaches, I had a rough idea of where they were in the range. I texted the wife that I won't be home until after dark, I am heading to the New Mexico border.

The Sangre de Cristo Range was something that words cannot describe. It is by far my favorite range in the state from the ground, and now occupies that spot from the air. The peaks rapidly rise up to 7,000 feet from a surrounding valley, a dry former lakebed that is flat as a pancake. Most ranges in the state have some sort of process where they progressively get to elevation, as opposed to such a near vertical presence. To top the entire experience off, there were low clouds that were in the small valleys between peaks on the range, making it an experience and a series of photographs one could not ever expect.

Blanca Peak from San Luis Valley

I passed along the beautiful range and over Great Sand Dunes National Park, down to the peaks around Blanca Peak. I had first laid eyes on these mountains in 2005 from the ground, and wanted to fly around them since. That goal was now fulfilled. It is truly a stunning series of peaks south of Great Sand Dunes, all in its own right, and in its own style.

The last one in this flight was Culebra Peak, down near the New Mexico border. Without the 14ers map, I had a rough idea where it was and photographed everything I saw. There was one clear prominence, though I had a hard time believing it was a 14er. It just didn't seem appropriately as dramatic. Further research showed that the timberline is well over 1,000' higher this far south, thus confusing the apparent majesty I was expecting. The amount of peak above the trees was far less.

The return trip took awhile, all told over 3 hours of flying in harsh, wickedly cold air. When I came back to land, I could barely feel my feet and had to extricate myself from the aircraft like I was literally frozen. It took a few hours to loosen up, rehydrate, and become human again. Some post-flight troubleshooting of the engine indicated an ignition problem had developed, so the aircraft ended up being down for maintenance for a few months as the issue was sourced and fixed. As is usual with airplane engines, they provide some bit of a warning that something is brewing, and the finicky mixture requirements were indicative of what turned out to be a very rare and bizarre malfunction of the magneto, requiring overhaul.

Rocky Mountain National Park

When the airplane finally was back in one piece, the next flight was to get Longs Peak, a forlorn single peak hiding in the northeast section of the mountains, far from any other 14er, and logistically impractical to combine with anything else. It required a 90-minute one-way flight to get there, with quite some wind along the way. It was my most harrowing takeoff at Leadville yet. As I cleared 200 feet above the ground, I hit a downdraft and began descending while at full power, with the airspeed indicator reading 38mph. I settled back into the nose high configuration, already on approach to land back down on the runway (at full power) and then the winds changed and I was climbing again. A rotor had worked its way 10 miles from Mt. Elbert over to the airfield. Most modern aircraft would have had to push the nose forward to avert a stall, making it a dramatic situation to avoid the ground at the same time. Cubs have such a high lift ratio that the air coming off the engine effectively prevents a full stall; the airplane merely descends. I had to find the location of the updraft section of the rotor to get any altitude, and use some creative techniques to climb along the ridgelines to get altitude. It was the most problematic day yet trying to climb out of Leadville, until I finally got altitude over Climax Mine and crossed the Tenmile Range.

When I finally did get to the Continental Divide, there were clouds. Not to be deterred, I pressed on toward Longs Peak and found that it was visible. The clouds were forming at the ridge and moving east, where they would become angry thunderstorms over the plains. I weaved around them and found Longs Peak attempting to hide from my camera. The photographs had a special mysticism being above the clouds and proved to be worth it. Rocky Mountain National Park featured aggressive terrain, providing a psychological baptism into the mindset of planning both surviving an unplanned landing and surviving the terrain afterwards. I followed the Colorado River on the return flight home for another project, and after having landed at Kremmling for fuel, I realized I had finally figured out the trick to cruising and enjoying the flight like I used to at lower altitudes. It is a careful subconscious tracking of where the winds are, what they should be doing, what they are doing instead, and working the throttle to keep the flight gentle and pleasant.

Independence Pass (12,095')

It became time to conquer the 14ers of the Elk Mountains. Winds had been rather strong, and a window of decent weather finally opened to tackle the trip. On this particular day, thunderstorms were forecast over the peaks, and I intended to also photograph a section of the Colorado River, so it was a matter of timing – hoping to get past the high peaks area before noon to avoid any nasty weather.

Milky Way from Independence Pass

As I climbed through Twin Lakes, I passed over Independence Pass, where I had taken some photographs after snowshoeing at night up a ridge to 12,800'. Truly a remarkable place, it was surprisingly docile from the air compared to some of the terrain I was about to embark on.

The Elk Mountains are rather severe, such that landing above timberline is generally not going to be a viable option in the event of engine failure. Most sections afforded the opportunity to glide within a reasonable enough range to Aspen that survival in the wilderness was not an issue, except it was quite rough near Maroon Peak and over toward Capitol Peak, what I am told is the hardest 14er ascent in the state. The entire exercise of flying in these expanses of death is a constant tracking of what few locations exist to land, and what direction to go to get out of the wilderness. On top of all of that, I am photographing and flying in turbulent air. After returning from these adventures, I am usually completely worn out and have to spend the rest of the day to recharge physically and mentally, though every bit is worth it.

The final flight was the San Juans. They are the farthest, and also appeared to be the most inhospitable. Peaks are in sections that make the Elk Mountains look like a cakewalk – 10 mile+ hikes to the nearest road, not necessarily the nearest piece of civilization. I initially photographed San Luis Peak, which is rather isolated and dry. This means that landing would have been fine, even on top of a peak. The hike out would not be deadly, simply very long. Umcompaghre and Wetterhorn Peaks were islands in the sky, surrounded by what looked like glaciers (and I know are not, merely residual snowpack from a very snowy year), and extremely isolated from any form of help. At least the

Elk Mountains

mountains around them were hospitable enough to permit a landing without certain death. These peaks were the farthest from civilization yet. My willpower was tested over Windom Peak and the associated 14ers around it. The terrain there is unlike any other in the rest of the state: extremely rough, spires of vertical rock, un-

Southern San Juan Mountains

forgiving valleys, extremely rugged terrain. That ruggedness translated into a beating in the air, with the airplane getting tipped left and right to very severe degrees, simply due to wind patterns. Trying to photograph was a real challenge, and I was quite uncomfortable with being over that terrain. I remember thinking "I am never doing this again." That is usually a sign that I somehow will, so stay tuned until I get the idea to do something silly there again.

El Diente Peak was fairly innocuous after Windom and its buddies. I came over a ridgeline into the valley around Telluride and then passed north to Mt. Sneffels, the final peak of the project. It also was benign in that it was isolated and I could glide down to Telluride airport if need be. After completing those photographs, I had the warmest feeling of satisfaction one could imagine. I had done it! The 14ers were photographed, a project of incredible magnitude. Smiling quite happily, I landed at Telluride to fuel up.

As I taxied toward the terminal area, I passed a small airliner loading passengers. The gawking was priceless on the part of the passengers, looking at that antique "thing" taxiing by. When I went in the terminal, a corporate jet pilot noted the aircraft and commented, "You flew in here with a Cub? You're nuts." He, of course, thought I flew into the valley like a normal pilot would. When I advised I came over a 13,000' ridge after photographing the 14ers, he was speechless.

After "completing" the project, I squirreled myself away into my office to begin the equally as challenging prospect of putting the book together, requiring not only the writing and organization of it, also the process of digging through all of the photos, identifying the peaks, post processing and the like. In the process, I could not find a good photo of two 14ers: Mt. Sherman and Mt. Bross. In an act of profound retardation, I failed to get a decent shot of the closest two to the airport. By this point, I was in the process of moving to the next adventure out of state. Thankfully, I had to return and get the airplane for the long flight out, so I was able to get both of these peaks on a cold summer morning flight in July.

After the actual completion of the project, it became evident that each flight was not just a piece of the overall puzzle, it was an experience in and of itself. I started with flights that I could handle safely with my flying skill, knowledge, and experience, and each additional flight increased all of those abilities. By progressively pushing my personal limits further, I had become a better and more resilient pilot all around, carefully refining my approach to remove unnecessary fears and to strengthen ones that belonged. I was no longer dominated by the drama of inexperience and ignorance; the days of imaginary demons lurking behind mountain peaks with spears were gone. I have asked if the process is simply an acceleration of normal pilot experience building, and I find that isn't the case. Many pilots have a goal to fly faster, with greater precision, on time, and safely, with our entire commercial airline system built on those foundations. No where in that framework do the limits get pushed intentionally, they do so only occasionally when protocols fail the pilot and suddenly the aircraft is in a mechanical or meteorological situation that had always been sought to be avoided. Adventure and bush flying is far different than the precision of airline travel, yet it is those that push the frontiers of engineering, skill, and aeronautical environment that help to progressively push the refined and precise boundaries of the normal. Behind every pleasant airline flight is a history book filled with test pilots and airplane designers who have pushed the boundaries one step further. I would recommend that each pilot be tasked with the duty to push the boundaries of aviation, as I am certain that the experienced gained in such harsh conditions serves the pilot and the community well. With only a handful of pilots living above 9,000 feet, and with 5 aircraft based at Leadville, I doubt many will play with these 14ers.

Sangre de Cristo Range

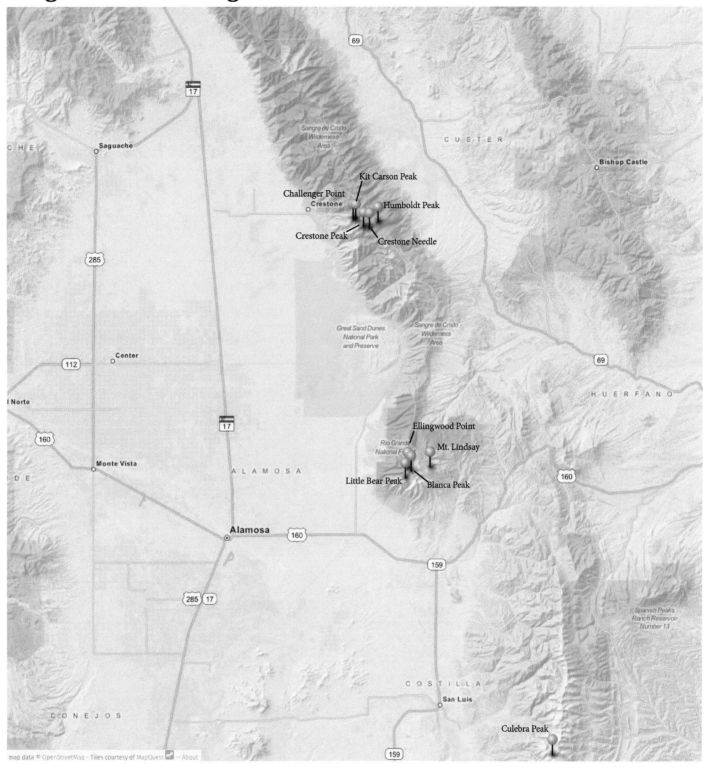

Page 88 & 89	SE	Sangre de Cristo Range
Page 90 & 91	E	Challenger Point (Left), Kit Carson Peak (Center), Crestone Peak & Crestone Needle (Center Rear), Humboldt Peak (Rear Left)
Page 92 & 93	E	Crestone Peak & Crestone Needle (Center), Humboldt Peak (Left)
Page 94	ESE	Challenger Point, Kit Carson Peak, Crestone Peak, Crestone Needle, Humboldt Peak (Distant)
Page 95	SE	Mt. Lindsey (Left Rear), Ellingwood Point (Center), Blanca Peak (Rear Right)
Page 96 & 97	SE	Great Sand Dunes National Park
Page 98 & 99	SE	Mt. Lindsdey (Center Left Rear), Ellingwood Point & Blanca Peak (Center Right Rear), Little Bear Peak (Right Rear)
Page 100 & 101	NE	Little Bear Peak (Front), Blanca Peak (Center), Ellingwood Point (Left), Mt. Lindsey (Center Rear)
Page 102 & 103	W	Little Bear Peak (Left), Blanca Peak (Center)
Page 104 & 105	SE	Culebra Peak
Page 106	SE	Culebra Peak

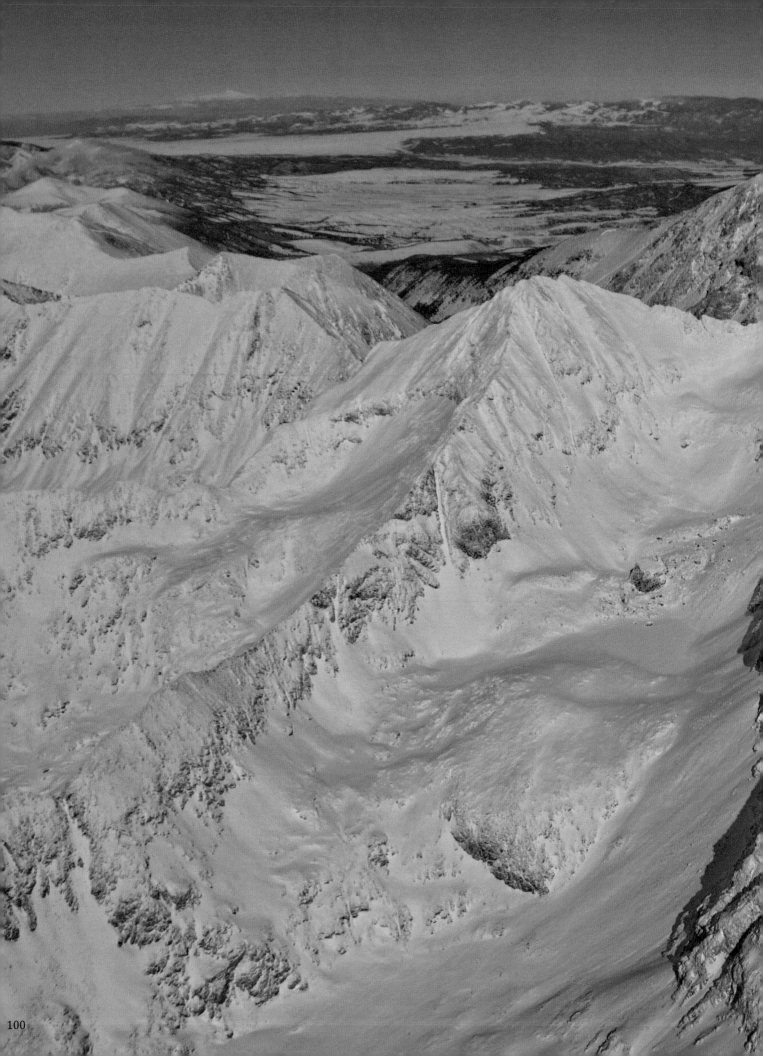

San Juan Mountains

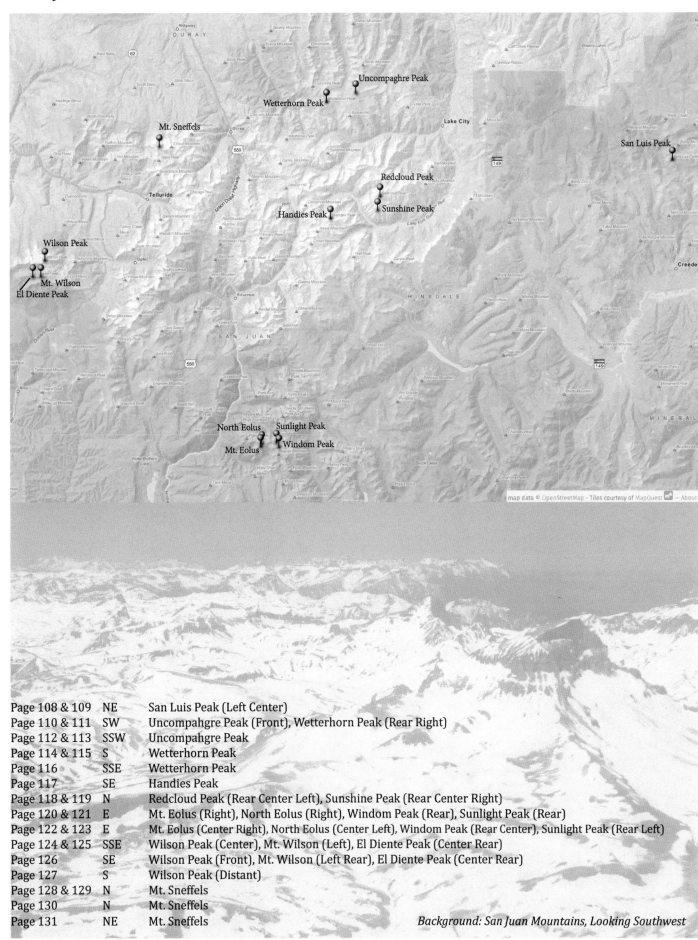

Page 108 & 109	NE	San Luis Peak (Left Center)
Page 110 & 111	SW	Uncompahgre Peak (Front), Wetterhorn Peak (Rear Right)
Page 112 & 113	SSW	Uncompahgre Peak
Page 114 & 115	S	Wetterhorn Peak
Page 116	SSE	Wetterhorn Peak
Page 117	SE	Handies Peak
Page 118 & 119	N	Redcloud Peak (Rear Center Left), Sunshine Peak (Rear Center Right)
Page 120 & 121	E	Mt. Eolus (Right), North Eolus (Right), Windom Peak (Rear), Sunlight Peak (Rear)
Page 122 & 123	E	Mt. Eolus (Center Right), North Eolus (Center Left), Windom Peak (Rear Center), Sunlight Peak (Rear Left)
Page 124 & 125	SSE	Wilson Peak (Center), Mt. Wilson (Left), El Diente Peak (Center Rear)
Page 126	SE	Wilson Peak (Front), Mt. Wilson (Left Rear), El Diente Peak (Center Rear)
Page 127	S	Wilson Peak (Distant)
Page 128 & 129	N	Mt. Sneffels
Page 130	N	Mt. Sneffels
Page 131	NE	Mt. Sneffels

Background: San Juan Mountains, Looking Southwest

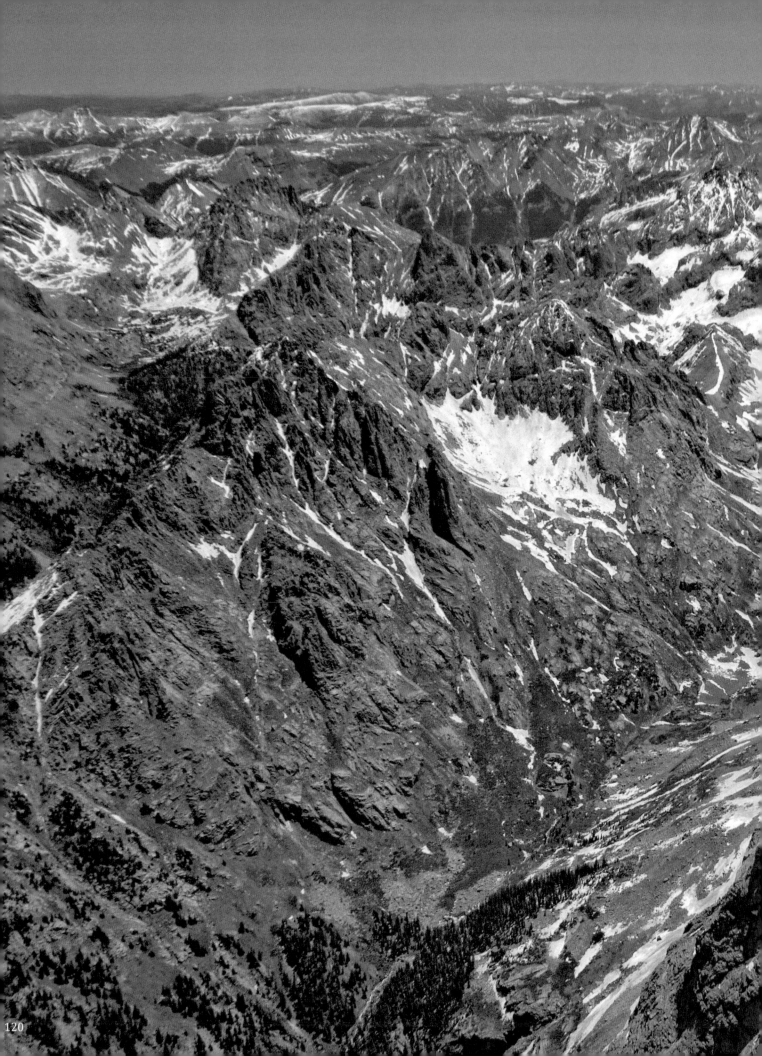

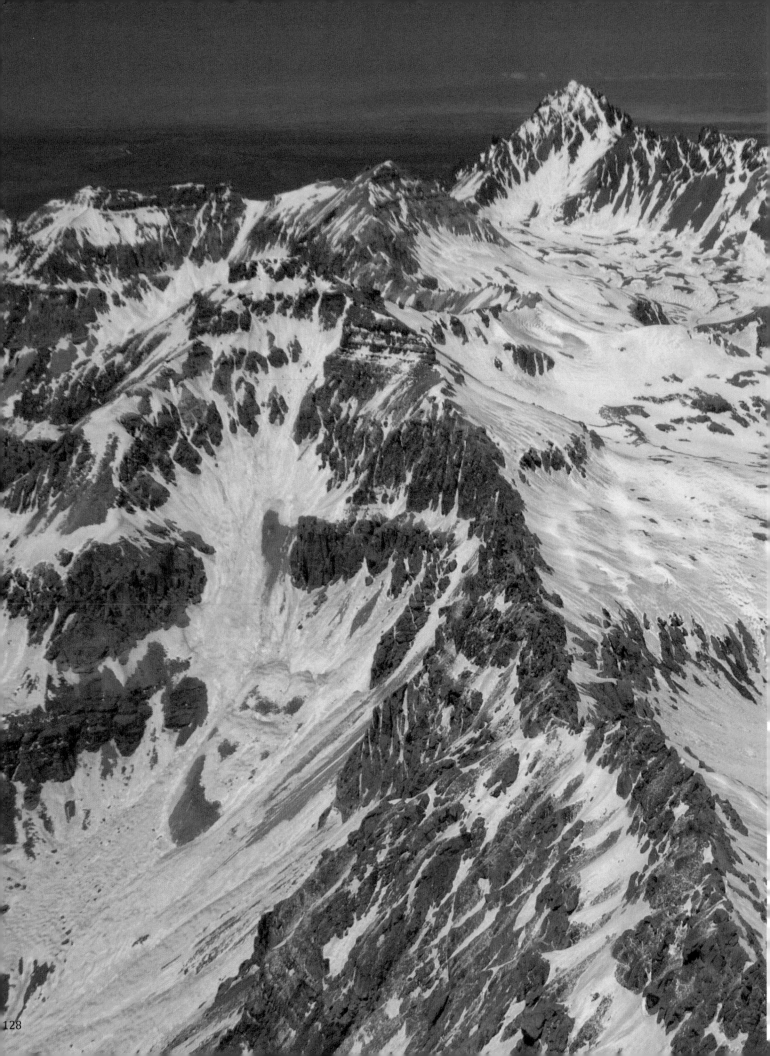

39118665R00075

Made in the USA
Lexington, KY
07 February 2015